THE TAO OF BRIDGE

200 Principles to Transform Your Game and Your Life

Brent Manley,
Author of *The Everything® Bridge Book*

Adams Media
Avon, Massachusetts

Published by
Adams Media, an F+W Publications Company
57 Littlefield Street, Avon, MA 02322. U.S.A.
www.adamsmedia.com

ISBN: 1-59337-216-7

Printed in Canada.

J I H G F E D C B A

Library of Congress Cataloging-in-Publication Data
Manley, Brent.
The tao of bridge / Brent Manley.
p.   cm.
ISBN 1-59337-216-7
1. Contract bridge—Moral and ethical aspects. 2. Duplicate contract
bridge—Moral and ethical aspects. 3. Taoist ethics. I. Title.
GV1282.32.M36 2005
795.41'5—dc22
2004013348

This book is available at quantity discounts for bulk purchases.
For information, call 1-800-872-5627.

Dedication

This book is dedicated to my wife, Donna.
She is my inspiration, motivation—and my favorite bridge partner.
We met through bridge and, as partners,
have enjoyed some significant triumphs at the table.

I also dedicate this to my father, Brent Manley, Sr.
He taught me the value of hard work and the
importance of doing your best at all times.

Lastly, I dedicate this book to my marathon running friends:
Bruce, Jackye, Lynlee, and Steve.
They inspire me to go the extra mile and to never give up.

Contents

Introduction

There is no question that as you progress in the wonderful game of bridge, your view of things will change. If you are like me, you will never lose your sense of wonder at perhaps the most fascinating, frustrating game you could possibly take up. As you become more expert, however, some principles of bidding and play will seem amazingly obvious to you—second nature, if you will. If you have much contact with newer players, it will behoove you to try to remember your early days in the game, when many of these bedrock principles were not so easy to grasp. The reason there are more than 5,000 bridge teachers in North America is that certain crucial concepts are not intuitively understood. Instruction and explanation are necessary.

In that sense, bridge mirrors life much more closely than you might imagine. When I look back on certain stages of my life, I'm amazed at my nearly complete lack of understanding—or even awareness—of various concepts that are very easy to grasp now. I wish there had been someone with me earlier in my life to sit me down and explain things in a way I could have readily understood and embraced.

The goal of this book is not to teach bridge. It's assumed you know the rudiments of the game—dealing the cards, counting your high-card points, taking finesses, etc. The objective is to help you progress more quickly in your understanding and acceptance of principles that may seem arcane or overly complicated but that are vital to your successful progression from newcomer to expert. Believe it or not, if you embrace bridge and master these important principles, there won't be much of a difference between you and the player who won a world championship last week. Believing in yourself is one of the elements that makes for success, whether it's at the local bridge club or the world championships.

You will find many references in this book to duplicate, the kind of bridge you encounter at most bridge clubs and at tournaments. This is because duplicate is by far the most interesting form of the game—for a variety of reasons you will note as you read on.

Bridge is a partnership game. You cannot play without another person sitting across the table from you. Much of what is written, therefore, will pertain to your relationship to that other person. Success in life—personal relations, your career—depends in large measure on how you relate to others, so the principles we identify as important for bridge will have corollaries in life.

You may be aware that Tao literally means "the way." This book is meant to show you the way to becoming a confident, skilled bridge player who lives life away from the table in a manner that others will try to emulate. Don't be put off by the various "don'ts" you find among these bridge principles. Where bad habits are concerned, you're much better off avoiding them in the first place.

You may be surprised at some of the advice you receive in this book. Keep your mind open. After all, that's the way to learn.

Chapter 1

A Game Unlike Any Other

As you circulate through the bridge world, you will meet a wide variety of people, from professionals to athletes to store clerks. The majority of them will tell you that once they discovered bridge, that was it for other games. Bridge has a way of latching on to you, of becoming addictive. Part of the reason is that, while it's pretty easy to learn to play, it's impossible to master the game. When you take up bridge, you are guaranteed a lifetime challenge.

➤ **Principle 1: Enjoy the endless variety of bridge.**

One of the fascinations of bridge is the endless number of combinations of the fifty-two cards in the deck. You could play bridge all day, every day for centuries and never see the same hand twice (the number of different combinations of the cards is a twenty-nine-digit number). Every deal is new, a potential adventure. If you appreciate the wonderful variety bridge offers, approaching the game with curiosity and a thirst for knowledge, you will be a successful player.

Your happiness is affected to a large extent by your view of life's unpredictability and your appreciation for the diversity of the experiences you can have by simply getting out of bed every day.

▷ **Principle 2: Appreciate the wonderful symmetry of bridge.**
There is a beautiful symmetry to the game of bridge that you do not see in other card games. The players are aligned according to the four compass points—North, South, East, and West—and the deal passes in a clockwise rotation, as do plays.

In many other card games, only part of the deck is used, imparting an element of luck to the play that does not exist in bridge. In bridge, all fifty-two of the cards are in play on every deal. Each player receives thirteen cards, and each player must contribute a card to each trick, so there are thirteen tricks in each deal. Thirteen is the magic number most players use to determine whether a hand is good enough to open the bidding. If you bid a grand slam, you must take all thirteen tricks. In setting up a bridge game, thirteen tables is considered an ideal movement because all the North-South pairs get to play all the East-West pairs.

There are many wonders in the world. Learn to appreciate them.

▷ **Principle 3: Appreciate the problem-solving aspects of bridge.**
Few things in life offer as much satisfaction as solving a problem. When you do it on your own, it is especially gratifying. The essence of bridge is solving problems. Experience will help you figure out exactly what problem you are attempting to solve. The form of scoring can influence the nature of the problem. In rubber bridge and team games, your objective is to make your contract. In a pair game, you might risk your contract for an overtrick. In some situations, you must determine whether there is a lie of the cards that will allow you to succeed. If so, you will try that solution no matter how unlikely it is to succeed.

♣ ♦ ♥ ♠

An active mind embraces the opportunity to solve problems.

➤ Principle 4: Enjoy the opportunities for surprise victories that bridge presents.

Few competitive endeavors allow a rank-and-file player to come face-to-face with a superstar—much less with a chance to win. You might enter the same road race as a world-class athlete, but if you are not at that elite level yourself, you have no chance of defeating the superior performer. Imagine taking the tennis court against Pete Sampras, or teeing it up with Tiger Woods. You might arrange something like that as an exhibition—if you have lots of money—but you would have no chance of winning.

In tournament bridge, you can buy an entry in the same event as a world champion. You can sit down at the table against the champion and his partner—and you have the opportunity to win. In a long match, the more experienced players will prevail most of the time. But in short matches or in a pair game—typically only two deals per round—you can come out ahead even against the top players in the world. If you play your cards correctly, there is nothing a top player can do about it. If luck is on your side and you don't chuck that advantage, you can win.

A well-rounded person enjoys life's opportunities.

➤ Principle 5: Be aware that bridge will present many challenges to players who want to improve.

It isn't enough to learn the ABCs of bidding and the various "rules" of card play—for example, "Always lead fourth from your longest and strongest suit against no-trump," or "Eight ever, nine never (when to finesse for a queen and when to play for the drop)." Many elements of bridge do not lend themselves to formulas, and you will have to teach yourself to think at the table. Learning percentages will help you to an extent, but you must strive to develop an awareness of when to ignore the odds.

As you play and progress, you will find yourself hitting plateaus—you're still trying hard but you don't seem to be getting better. You must counsel yourself that the effort will be rewarded eventually. When good habits become second nature, your mind will clear for more in-depth detective work. You will sweep emotion from your bridge psyche. Your silly mistakes will start to dwindle. Your confidence will grow. You will be a bridge player.

♣ ♦ ♥ ♠

*Bright people love challenges and are not easily deterred
from their goals for improving themselves.*

▷ **Principle 6: Accept that luck—good and bad—is a major force in bridge.**
It can't be quantified. No one has yet figured out how to bottle it. It can frustrate and confound you in bridge, as in other areas of your life. The fact is that luck is a huge factor in your success as a player. When you accept that and strive to maintain your equilibrium in the face of luck—good as well as bad—you will be on your way as a bridge player.

Luck can manifest itself in many ways in bridge. In a rubber bridge game, where the cards are shuffled and dealt again and again, the so-called run of the cards can have a profound effect on your success. If you get good cards—translation: lots of high cards—you most likely will win. If you get bad cards, you're going to lose. In tournament bridge, you will experience luck in an entirely different way. In a tournament, the deals are played again and again by all the competitors. You get your score from comparing how you did on a deal to the scores achieved on that same deal by all the others who played it. You can win, therefore, with bad cards by getting pluses despite the deals you get—or by recording smaller minuses than the other pairs.

There are literally hundreds of ways you can experience luck. For example, the opponents might have a bidding misunderstanding and fail to reach even game when they have all the tricks. It can work the other way as well, unfortunately: The opponents screw up the auction and fail to reach game when they have 29 HCP between them, only for you to find that bad breaks in all the suits make game impossible.

♣ ♦ ♥ ♠

You will not be judged by the good and bad fortune that comes your way but by your reaction to the whims of fate.

> **Principle 7: Play with many, but strive to develop at least one good partnership.**

It is wise to play with a variety of partners, not just to soak up their expertise when you are starting out, but also to find out about different concepts and approaches to problem-solving. You will learn about different conventions and bidding understandings by playing with a variety of people, giving you a chance to sample the complete buffet and make your choices based on your comfort level. For example, if you are a good bidder but not a strong dummy player, you will benefit from playing with someone whose declarer skills are advanced. There are many permutations of this concept. Don't underestimate the advantages of having a variety of partners.

Having said that, you should also try to find at least one person with whom you are willing to work to create a long-term partnership. It requires studying, keeping notes, and lots of bidding practice, but the reward can be great. Bridge is intriguing, frustrating, and completely fascinating. Playing bridge in a regular partnership can be incredibly satisfying as well. It is well known in expert circles that average players within well-oiled partnerships can often triumph over world-class players where bidding agreements and understandings are not well developed.

♣ ♦ ♥ ♠

Variety may be the spice of life, but there is value in the tried and true as well.
Happy people achieve a balance between the two.

➤ Principle 8: Enjoy the social aspects of bridge.

There are various ways to enjoy bridge. Many people play only at home, mostly for social reasons. There is a certain level of competition, but the focus is on getting together with friends.

Another common arena for bridge play is the rubber bridge game, distinguished from "party bridge" alluded to above by the fact that the participants are playing for money—sometimes a lot of it. Rubber bridge clubs are much more scarce today than in the 1940s, '50s, and early '60s, but there are still some famous ones, including a club in London called The Great Rose (after Irving Rose, a famous British player). There are also a couple of high-stakes clubs in New York City, and there are many high-stakes games going on all the time in homes or venues not strictly set up for bridge. These games are ultra-serious, and little socializing goes on.

Finally, there is duplicate, which combines "serious" bridge with the opportunity to socialize. The proprieties of bridge keep any talk during the bidding and play to a minimum, but duplicate clubs are social gathering places to be sure. If you play much bridge, you are likely to become friends with many of the people you meet at your local bridge club. Getting the maximum from the game of duplicate involves study and a competitive spirit, but you will do yourself a disservice if you ignore the opportunities to meet people. Being friendly and courteous will make you the type of person others will want to play with, expanding your horizons and increasing your enjoyment of the game.

Man is a social animal. Even the greatest of
successes means little if it is not shared with others.

Chapter 2

The Cards in Your Hand

Before video games and computers came along, it was customary for people to play cards. In the 1940s and '50s, card games were a common family activity. And, if you already had some familiarity with cards, learning to play bridge seemed easier. Many games, such as spades, gave participants a grounding in the concept of taking tricks. Today, many people who take up bridge are having their first experience with cards. That doesn't mean bridge is too tough for them to understand; it's just that they have to learn a bit more to get started.

> **Principle 9: Understand that the game of bridge is a game of tricks.**

It is important to never forget that your objective in the game of bridge is to take tricks. If you are in a contract of 4♠, you must always remember that your target is ten tricks. Keeping this uppermost in your consciousness will lead to good habits and a reputation as a tough adversary. Similarly, if the opponents are playing 3NT, you and partner must seek a way to take five tricks.

Bidding, as you will come to understand, is usually the most important phase of the game. It doesn't matter how well you play if you consistently miss the correct contract. On the other hand, you will flounder and fail if you are unable to take the tricks that belong to you (along with some that don't). A balanced approach to bridge is to try to learn bidding and play in equal measures. If you must sacrifice one for the other in starting out, put your emphasis on trick taking.

A safe arrival at your destination is much more important
than the route you take to get there.

▷ **Principle 10: All hands are not created equal.**
Spot cards and the alignment of high cards can have a significant effect on the value of a hand. Take the following hands, for example:

1. ♠A432	♥K76	♦Q32	♣J43
2. ♠A1098	♥K96	♦Q109	♣J106
3. ♠AKQJ76	♥876	♦54	♣72

All three have 10 high-card points, with the ace equaling 4, down to the jack at 1. Hand No. 1, however, might take only one trick (the spade ace), while Hand No. 3 is a favorite to take six tricks. Hand No. 2, with lots of 10s and 9s, has much better prospects, but it is still a much lesser hand than No. 3 because the honor cards are divided. Keep this idea in mind as you evaluate your hand.

You get much better results in your workplace and your life when you have all of
your assets working together rather than going separate ways.

▷ **Principle 11: Learn the right way to evaluate your assets.**
You now understand that high cards working in combination are more powerful than high cards working alone. You now also appreciate the difference between "chunky" suits and "empty suits." The former have lots of 10s and 9s to go with their high cards, the latter feature more 4s and 3s. Be careful, as well, about your evaluation

of so-called unguarded honors: singleton kings, doubleton queens, tripleton jacks. In fact, you are better served by not considering jacks unless they are in combination with other cards, such as AJ73 or QJ54. Some experts assign extra value to hands without queens, and it is axiomatic among experienced players that an ace is worth more than four on the high-card point scale. It is a mistake to assign points for distributional features—voids, singletons, doubletons—in the initial valuation of a hand. Shortness has no value unless a trump fit exists, and in fact can be a serious flaw in a hand in some situations. Singleton aces are often overvalued. It is true that possession of a singleton ace seems to provide the ultimate protection when you are playing in a suit contract, but there is no flexibility with a singleton ace. When the suit is led, you have to play it, precluding the often-effective first-round duck of the suit. Singleton aces are most definitely detriments for no-trump play, providing one and only one stopper with no possibility of a holdup play.

Take a cue from the saying, "All that glitters is not gold."
What might seem to be a valuable asset may be a liability.

▷ **Principle 12: To achieve the optimum in the bidding process, you must be prepared to re-evaluate your hand constantly as the auction proceeds.**
Say you are dealt the following hand:

♠KJ732   ♥K43   ♦KQJ6   ♣8

You would prefer to have at least one ace, but there are 13 high-card points and this is certainly a hand worth an opening bid, so you start with 1♠. When your left-hand opponent enters the auction with a bid of 2♥, everything changes. All of a sudden, your ♥K, evaluated at 3 high-card points initially, has dropped significantly in value. Why? Because it is very likely that the ♥A is on your left. In bridge parlance, the ♥A is "over" your king. When you first picked up your hand, that king was worth half a trick—it will win a trick opposite a poor holding any time the ace is to your right, which is about half the time. Now you know the prospects for taking a trick with that king are at about zero. Instead of a 13-point hand, it is now in effect a 10-point hand. Furthermore, the chances are increased that your left-hand opponent holds the ♦A. If so, your diamond holding is probably now worth only two tricks.

In normal circumstances, if you opened 1♠ with that hand and partner raised to 2♠, you might consider making a game-try bid of 3♦. Now, if partner raises you to 2♠ after the 2♥ overcall, you will go quietly. The value of your hand has changed and you must recognize this. It is losing bridge to fail to re-evaluate your assets as you gain information from the bidding.

♣ ♦ ♥ ♠

Life is a process, and things change as you move through it.
What is important or valuable to you today may be of no worth tomorrow.
Successful, happy people are willing to let go when it's necessary.

➤ **Principle 13: Learn to distinguish between "good" and "bad" high-card points.**
Just as hands are not created equal, neither are high-card points. In general, you want your HCP in your long suits. HCP in short suits, such as ♠KQ doubleton, may be useful for defense but will not provide many tricks on offense. Most experts do not have much use for the holding commonly known as a "quack"—the doubleton QJ of a suit. Those two together, although 3 HCP on paper, may take no tricks at all. If partner opens 1♠, showing at least five of them, and you hold ♠AJ543, your ♠J is essentially a wasted card. With so many trumps between the two hands, the ♠J is not really needed to bring in the suit. When partner reveals extreme shortness in a suit,

your HCP in that suit become "wasted" values, with one exception—the ace. Say you open 1♠ on the following hand:

♠AQJ54　　♥KQ　　♦KJ3　　♣652

Now let's say partner bids 4♦, showing a hand good enough to raise you to game in spades—with a singleton or a void in diamonds. This is known as a "splinter" and is a popular bidding tool among tournament players. The splinter is a valuable tool that can help you reach slam.

Holding the hand above, however, you are not at all excited to learn about the shortness in diamonds. That means that 4 of the HCP in your hand are "wasted." The chances are good that you will take only one trick in diamonds—and it's possible you will take none. Plus, you have to figure out how to get rid of the other losers. Yes, you can ruff them in partner's hand because you know he is short in diamonds, but that means you won't be able to draw trumps right away. You might still be able to make a slam if partner has exactly the right cards, but you'll be a loser in the long run if you go searching for slams with hands of this type.

But what if your hand was like the following?

♠AQJ54　　♥KQ　　♦6532　　♣KJ

When partner makes a splinter bid of 4♦, you love your diamond holding. You will most likely lose a trick in the suit, but you can also consider that, since partner has no HCP in diamonds, his other points will be "working" opposite your honors. Slam is a very real possibility.

♣ ♦ ♥ ♠

Amassing possessions just for the sake of having them is a poor way to live.
Try to find assets that will enhance your life.

> **Principle 14: Don't be a "point counter." Learn the value of "shape."**

Look carefully at the two hands below. Which would you prefer to hold?

    ♠KQ   ♥KQ4   ♦QJ43   ♣9652
  ♠AJ10765 ♥A10765   ♦7   ♣4

If you rely strictly on high-card points, you will look at the first deal and conclude that you have an opening bid with 13 HCP. You will see the second hand as "only" 9 HCP, so you might pass.

To be a successful player, you must understand that shape is much more important than points. With the two examples above, many players would pass with the second hand because "it only has nine points." That is folly. If partner can support either major, you will be a favorite to take a ton of tricks.

A truly extreme example of point-count mania occurred in a tournament in Nashville, Tennessee, during the 1990s. The four hands were as follows:

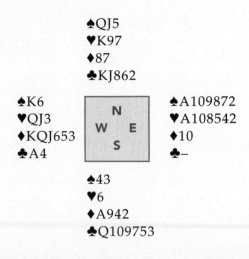

             ♠QJ5
             ♥K97
             ♦87
             ♣KJ862

♠K6   ♠A109872
♥QJ3   **N**   ♥A108542
♦KQJ653 **W**   **E**   ♦10
♣A4   **S**   ♣–

             ♠43
             ♥6
             ♦A942
             ♣Q109753

East was the dealer and this incredible auction took place.

W	N	E	S
		P	P
1♣	P	1♦	All Pass

Obviously, some explanation is necessary here. East-West were playing what is known as a strong club system. That is, the opening bid of 1♣ is artificial, showing a strong hand of usually 16 or more HCP. Furthermore, their agreement was that unless responder had 9 or more HCP, he was bound to respond 1♦, another artificial bid, indicating nothing more than HCP. Since East was a passed hand, and he could have no more than 8 HCP, West didn't see where the two hands were going (he could have raised to 2♦, but that would have only increased the level of the contract for no really good reason). Thus did East become declarer at 1♦ on a deal where he could easily take twelve tricks in hearts. At many tables in this particular game, East opened the bidding with 1♠ despite holding only 8 HCP. That is not at all unreasonable with such great shape. Even after East passed, however, he could still have evaluated his hand opposite partner's strong 1♣ opener as a "positive" response.

The above example may seem absurd, but it is repeated to a lesser extent in bridge games around the world as players rely on points for their bidding decisions rather than taking a closer look at the wonderful asset called shape.

It's a good idea to obey the law, but many of the "rules" you encounter are more guidelines than unbreakable standards. Learn to tell the difference.

▷ **Principle 15: Learn to appreciate the power of trumps.**
Early on, bridge players learn the value of trumps for ruffing. With trumps, you can stop the opponents from running a suit. Having

extra trumps, starting with the nine-card fit, means taking extra tricks. With only eight trumps—the so-called golden fit—you frequently are unable to draw trumps and ruff losers. With nine or more trumps, you have much more flexibility.

Having trump tricks is also important when the auction becomes competitive. Many a player has doubled an opponent's contract based on high-card points, only to see declarer romp home with a demoralizing crossruff. "But I had 15 points," does not satisfy partner as he chalks up minus 670 or 730.

The more trumps you and partner have between you, the fewer your opponents will have, meaning the high-card points in your trump suit diminish in trick-taking power. If you ever hear someone say, "That was a 30-point deck," it usually means one of the players was void in a suit held by the opponents. You may hold ♠AKQJ—that's 10 HCP—but if one of your opponents is void in that suit, your 10 HCP will take exactly zero tricks. For the opponents, it's a 30-point deck rather than the usual 40.

*Sometimes, your smallest assets can become
your most useful and valuable possessions.*

Chapter 3

Bidding—The Language of Bridge

Most expert players will tell you that bidding is the most important element of bridge. If you consistently arrive at the wrong contract, you will consistently underachieve. It doesn't matter how well you play if you can't manage to find the optimum contract—or close to it—most of the time. Good contracts don't just happen. They are the product of good bidding.

▶ **Principle 16: Cultivate an understanding of how bidding works.**
The form of bridge that you play is technically known as contract bridge. It evolved from the old English game called whist. In the 1920s, millionaire Harold Vanderbilt introduced a change in the scoring of what was then known as auction bridge. Before that change, bidding was not such an important element of the game. If you bid 1♥ and made all thirteen tricks, you got the same score as if you had bid 7♥. Vanderbilt's innovation put more emphasis on accuracy—unless you bid a game or slam, you didn't get credit for it.

The "contract" element is simple: When the auction is completed, one side has contracted to take a certain number of tricks. If that contract is not fulfilled, there is a penalty.

From the time of Vanderbilt's innovation forward, bidding has become the most important element of bridge. Bidding is your way of talking to your partner—and vice versa—and there are only fifteen words you can use: the numbers one through seven, the four suits, no-trump, double, redouble, and pass. You are not allowed to say anything else about your hand in any other way.

Bridge is still a game of tricks, but as more and more players gain bidding expertise, it is vitally important for you to keep up. Even if you aren't interested in playing certain bidding conventions (another way of describing a specific agreement as to the meaning of a certain bid), it will behoove you to become familiar with all the weapons your opponents will be using so that you can cope with them.

*If you have a natural curiosity about how things work,
you will be better prepared for a new endeavor.*

▶ Principle 17: Do not underestimate the importance of bidding.

You may never go to a tournament or play duplicate at a club, but if you make no effort to learn proper bidding, you will always have a sense—vague though it may be—that you could be doing more, doing better. If you and partner have no idea what your bids mean, you will not enjoy bridge to its fullest. You will tire of finding yourself in 4♦, taking all the tricks, and wondering how you could have bid the two hands properly. You will bid slams and watch the opponents, right off the bat, cash two aces or the ace and king of a suit as you try to suppress the feeling that this disaster should not have happened. And that's just for those who stick to party bridge.

If you venture to a duplicate club and eventually to a tournament, you will find yourself continually at the bottom of the standings if you do not learn to bid. It's not necessary for you to play the most sophisticated systems or the latest conventions and gadgets. You must, however, have a sound foundation in the rudiments of the auction. You may be the best dummy player you know—as many former rubber bridge players are when they gravitate to duplicate—but if you are constantly in the wrong contract, your scores will reflect your deficiencies. Remember that in tournaments you get your score from comparing your score to that of the others who played your hand.

Here's an example of how you can go wrong if you don't understand simple nuances and how important it is to be able to accurately describe your assets. Say you hold the following hand:

♠J4   ♥KQ1097   ♦K107   ♣843

Partner opens 1NT, showing 15–17 high-card points. It's generally accepted that you can make game with 25 HCP, although some bidding books suggest 26 HCP for the minimum. Stick to 25 and you will be fine. At any rate, this hand is on the borderline. If partner has 16 or 17 HCP, you want to be in game. If partner has only 15 HCP, you want to play a part score. Looking more closely at the hand, you are impressed with your fine heart suit. That could be a source of tricks for partner, but since you have only five hearts, you cannot insist on a suit contract. If you play out-of-date methods, you are in a pickle with this hand. Your only real invitational bid is 2NT, but if you bid that, partner might have:

♠Q6   ♥A832   ♦AQ65   ♣K92

If so, he will pass and the opponents will take the first five spade tricks, plus at least one trick in clubs (perhaps many more). 2NT will be a dreadful contract.

If you decide to evaluate your hand aggressively and bid 3♥ (forcing to game and giving partner the choice between 3NT and 4♥), partner will turn up with

♠A653   ♥65   ♦AQ4   ♣KQ76

Partner would struggle to make 3NT, and 4♥ would have almost no play.

So perhaps you should bid 2♥, a so-called drop-dead bid? Well, if you do that, partner will turn up with

♠A6　　♥A832　　♦AQ65　　♣K92

Now game in hearts would be a reasonable proposition, but you are languishing in 2♥.

The solution is an elementary part of duplicate—the Jacoby transfer, named after Oswald Jacoby, its creator and one of bridge's all-time greats.

With the hand in question, you would bid 2♦, transferring to hearts, then you would follow with a bid of 2NT, showing invitational values and a five-card heart suit (with six, you would transfer and bid 3♥). This has the dual value of allowing for an invitational sequence that identifies a major-suit fit when one exists—and protecting the assets of the strong hand.

Lest you get the idea that this book is heading for bidding lessons, relax. The point is that a bit of sophistication in the bidding is absolutely necessary for success.

♣ ♦ ♥ ♠

For any job you undertake, be sure you have the right tools.

➤ Principle 18: Understand that every bid has a meaning.

This may seem such an obvious statement that it is out of place in this book. Far from it. If you are to succeed at bridge, you must understand that every call you make carries a message to partner. You know, of course, that in the language of the auction every bid is a call, but not every call is a bid (pass, double, and redouble are calls but are not bids). Thus, as the auction progresses, you impart information to partner (and, alas, to the opponents, but you can't help that) in every move you make. If you do not understand this, you are headed for trouble.

A common mistake of developing players is to make a bid or call that denies a certain holding that is actually possessed—some number of cards or some high-card strength—followed by a later attempt to "untell" the story just told. This can cause disaster.

For example, suppose your hand is

♠AK10   ♥J654   ♦QJ98   ♣85

Partner opens 1♣ and you decide to let partner know you have a balanced hand with 11 or 12 HCP. For most modern players, a bid of no-trump over an opening of one of a minor denies a four-card major. You suppress your heart suit because it's not too strong. When partner's next bid is 3♣, declining your game invitation and describing an unbalanced hand not suitable for no-trump, you start to worry that maybe you are missing a fit in hearts that could produce a game. For example, partner's hand might be as follows:

♠4   ♥A1098   ♦A5   ♣A109764

If this is the hand, you will have excellent play for a game contract in hearts. The only problem is, you can't get there from where you are. You have already denied a four-card major with your bid of 2NT. If you try hearts now, it will only confuse partner.

There's an old bridge story about two players, one of whom did not apparently understand the concept advanced here. When the bidding was over and dummy was putting down his hand, the declarer inquired in alarm: "Partner, where is the hand you held during the bidding?" If you do not take into account what your bids mean so that your bidding accurately reflects what you have, you are setting yourself up for failure.

♠ ♦ ♥ ♠

Your relationships—with friends, family, and business associates—
will be much more rewarding if you always tell the truth.

➢ Principle 19: Learn to pass.

Bridge is a bidder's game to be sure, but you will know you have
arrived as a player when you learn to pass as well.

Say you are playing in a tournament and you pick up the following hand:

♠A4   ♥QJ4   ♦AJ1076   ♣753

You open 1♦, your left-hand opponent passes, partner bids 1♠,
and the next player bids 2♥. Now what? Let's increase the level of
risk by saying that your side is vulnerable, meaning that if you go
set, it might be a very big number.

Your 1♦ opener might have been made on three low diamonds—you do that sometimes when you are playing five-card
major openers—so your natural inclination is to show that you
actually have a diamond suit. How will partner know you have
diamonds if you don't say something now? The urge to bid 3♦ is
like an itch that needs to be scratched. You might get away with it if
you bid 3♦ here, but if you do, you will be describing a hand much
stronger than the one you hold. You will also be describing a hand
with six or more diamonds. You have only five.

A pass with this hand is about as clear-cut as anything gets
in bridge. Remember, you have a partner over there. If you pass,
he will know a couple of things about your hand: You don't have
as many as three spades, because if you did, you would probably
have raised to 2♠. That would not show anything extra and would
not promise more than three spades. If you pass, partner will know
you don't have a hand strong enough to make a penalty double

of 2♥; he will know you don't have a bit extra with extra length in diamonds, or you would have bid 3♦. That's a lot of information you have conveyed simply by passing.

Also, just because partner bid doesn't mean it's your hand. If he has some values and a diamond fit, he can still bid.

♣ ♦ ♥ ♠

A wise, disciplined person overcomes temptation and sticks to the correct path.

➤ Principle 20: Find a bidding system you are comfortable with and stick to it.

When it comes to bidding systems, it's a real cafeteria out there. Many older players learned Goren standard, named for Charles Goren, whose name is still synonymous with bridge. The system, however, features four-card major openings and is now considered pretty much old-fashioned and dated. There is Standard American, featuring fifteen to seventeen 1NT openers, five-card majors, and a few gadgets, such as transfers over no-trump and negative doubles. An adjunct of Standard American is the method known as two-over-one game force, referred to mostly as 2/1. The principal feature is that if one player opens the bidding and responder bids at the two level, the two-level bid, in theory at least, is forcing to game. The system is efficient inasmuch as you don't have to go jumping around when partner makes a 2/1 response. On the other hand, when partner opens 1♠ and the main feature of your hand is a seven-card club suit, it doesn't feel right to bid 1NT (the book bid if you don't have an opening hand yourself) instead of mentioning your clubs.

There are also strong club systems (a 1♣ opener is artificial, showing 16 or more HCP), Kaplan-Sheinwold, featuring a "weak" 1NT opener (12–14) and myriad other systems. Through the years, literally hundreds of homemade systems have sprung up, most of them curiosities but not worth inspecting.

One factor that will determine your comfort level with a bidding system is your willingness to memorize agreements and conventions. Another will be your ability to remember all that you are playing in the heat of competition. Those who are starting out will be much happier if they don't burden themselves with a lot of memory work.

♣ ♦ ♥ ♠

*In any undertaking, it is best to not to bite off more
than you can chew in the early going.*

➤ Principle 21: Remember the importance of complete discussion of your methods with your partner before you play.

This applies mostly to duplicate or tournament players, but there is merit in discussing your methods even if you aren't playing anything sophisticated or complex. Your partner might want to know, for example, your style when it comes to preemptive bidding. For example, are you likely to open 3♣ on a six-card suit? What can partner expect when you open a weak 2♠? If you raise 1♥ directly to 3♥, what does that mean? If you open 1NT and partner bids Stayman (asking for a four-card major), do you bid hearts first if you have both majors? Do you play any variations of Blackwood (the ace-asking bid)? When does Gerber (another ace-asking convention) apply?

Granted, there are many approaches considered standard, but you will see a lot of different interpretations, and there is nothing more frustrating than having bidding accidents on relatively straightforward bids.

At clubs and tournaments, you and your partner must fill out a convention card—a list of the agreements your partnership is employing in the bidding. Go over it point by point as you fill it out. You will find the time well spent.

♣ ♦ ♥ ♠

If you fail to prepare, you are preparing to fail.

➤ Principle 22: Be disciplined.

If you want to be a good player, you will need some imagination and creativity. You are free, within the proprieties of the game, to deceive your opponents—by your bids and plays but not by your mannerisms or comments. That said, aspiring players must also recognize that discipline is a key to long-term success.

A disciplined bridge player always bids within the agreed-upon system. If the partnership parameters for a weak two-bid are two of the top three honors in the suit, a disciplined player will never open 2♦ on

| ♠54 | ♥Q4 | ♦KJ10983 | ♣654 |

If an opening bid with a balanced hand shows two and a half quick tricks, a disciplined player will pass with

| ♠J54 | ♥AQ109 | ♦K43 | ♣Q62 |

A disciplined player does not "fight it out" with partner when his and partner's hands are obviously misfits.

A disciplined player strives to maintain concentration, stops to think before making an "obvious" play, and watches partner's cards for help on defense.

Adopting a disciplined style may cost you an occasional lucky outcome, but you will be a winner in the long run and a sought-after partner if you are known as a player who always has his bids.

♣ ♦ ♥ ♠

Learning discipline is not easy, but the rewards can be great.

➤ Principle 23: An undisciplined style has its rewards—and drawbacks.

There is no question that you can wreak havoc with an undisciplined bidding style, particularly when it comes to preemptive bidding—and it will pay you to remember that your job is to make life as difficult for the opponents as you can. If you give the opponents a free ride every time they have the majority of the high-card points, their bidding will be depressingly accurate.

You will increase the opponents' anxiety, for example, if you make it a practice to open a weak two-bid on any hand with a six-card suit, regardless of its composition. For example, 2♠ on a hand such as

    ♠J96543   ♥K4   ♦J87   ♣Q5

This can cause severe problems for an opponent holding something like

    ♠Q7   ♥AJ87   ♦KQ543   ♣KJ

The high-card points are sufficient for a 2NT overcall (showing the same HCP as you would have for a 1NT opener), but the hand has no spade stopper. If you double with this hand and partner bids clubs, he could be playing a 4-2 fit at the three level. If you overcall 3♦ with that moth-eaten suit (which you probably should), you could be doubled, going down several tricks. There no question that the 2♠ bid made your life miserable.

While it may please you to throw such monkey wrenches into your opponents' auctions, remember this: Your partner also has to cope with your undisciplined bids.

If the two of you believe that preemption and interference outweigh the bad results you will get from an undisciplined style, go for it. There is no question that crazy bidders are difficult to deal with. Experienced players, however, know that the best antidote for such a style is the single word "double." Plus 1100 can go a long way toward easing your feelings of anxiety about the opponents' wild bidding style.

♣ ♦ ♥ ♠

You can be happy marching to the beat of a different drummer if you understand and accept that it will not always be easy to live that way.

Chapter 4

The Opening Bid—
Getting in the First Shot

Seizing the initiative is almost always a good idea. There's a lot to that saying about the early bird and the worm. When you strike the first blow in a bridge game by opening the bidding, you make the opponents' task that much harder. Their bidding becomes much less precise. You should not strain to open, but don't pass up any reasonable opportunity.

> **Principle 24: It's important to open if you can.**

The side that opens the bidding has a decided advantage in the auction. For starters, the side that opens has seized the initiative. Even if the opening bid shows a weak hand, such as a preemptive bid of 3♣—you have started describing your hand to partner, who now has information he can use to find the right spot. In many ways, the lower-level bids—what you might call regular, opening hands of 12 high-card points or more—can be more preemptive than the higher-level bids describing weaker hands.

    This is particularly true of the spade suit. If you open 1♠, unless an opponent can overcall 1NT, any direct bid over that opener must be at the two level. Bidding at the two level can be dangerous when the vulnerability is in the opponents' favor, so the opening bid has already gained advantage in many cases.

Further, it is fairly standard for a balanced opener to contain a certain number of quick tricks, usually two to two and a half. That's information that can be very useful if the auction becomes competitive.

Think of the opening bid as you would a serve in tennis. The server always has an advantage.

♣ ♦ ♥ ♠

The race is not always to the swift.
Sometimes, the winners are those who seize the initiative.

> **Principle 25: Understand the tradeoffs of adhering to "sound" openers.**

One of the challenges of bridge is walking that fine line between safety and aggression. You want to get in that first shot, but if your dummies are more often disappointing than inspiring, there will be trouble for your partnership. This is especially true if you play 2/1 game force. That is, if you open at the one level and your partner makes a two-level response (as an unpassed hand), you and partner cannot stop bidding until you reach game.

If you play 2/1 and open light, as more and more players these days are wont to do, you are in for trouble, especially if no fit is found and you end up in no-trump. Consider the following hand:

♠AK765   ♥A543   ♦732   ♣6

Just about anyone would open that hand, despite the fact that it has "only" 11 HCP. There are three quick tricks, a handy rebid after an opener of 1♠, and shortness should partner fit one of your majors.

It's not so good, however, if partner has something like the following:

♠J2   ♥Q7   ♦KQ654   ♣AJ54

That's 13 HCP, and you have a perfectly normal bid of 2♦ over partner's 1♠ opener, but you have no major-suit fit, and you will need to be very lucky to make 3NT. If the ♦A is in the wrong place, you have virtually no shot at nine tricks in no-trump.

Does that mean that it is wrong to open 1♠ with the 11-point hand? Probably. If you could be certain you would be able to play a suit contract, it would not be a problem. But if you are not in a position to insist on a suit—perhaps you would be if you had five cards in each major instead of five of one and four of the other—so you are better off taking it easy.

Balanced hands present even more danger. When your shape is dull, you rarely have the opportunity to ruff anything, meaning your tricks must be taken with high cards. If you are short of high cards, you will often find yourself in dire straits.

It is true that if you agree to open only with "sound" values—aces and kings, cards in combination rather than scattered assets—you will give up some of that valuable "initiative" you want to seize.

The flip side of that is that if partner must continually allow for the fact that your opener might be suspect, you will lose a lot of bidding accuracy and the partnership's confidence level will deteriorate.

Every decision we make, every position we take, has a consequence.
You are much better off if you think things through ahead
of time and prepare yourself for possible reactions.

> **Principle 26: It sometimes pays to go against the flow.**

In duplicate bridge, you can sometimes gain a lot by being different—making a conscious decision to do what is unlikely to be done at most other tables. This requires some general knowledge of players' tendencies and the bidding systems they play, but you will learn most of what you need to know simply by playing. If you are observant, you will get a feel for what the average player tends to do.

There are various ways to, as it were, swim upstream. One of them is to adjust the range of your 1NT openers, usually to what is known as the "weak no-trump," an opening of 1NT showing 11–14 or 12–14 HCP. Some even go so far as to open 1NT with 10–12 HCP when they are not vulnerable. These openings often have the contracts played from the "other" side of the table. In other words, if most North-South pairs playing a no-trump contract will have it played by South, the weak no-trump opening can result in North's playing the contract. This can have a profound effect on the outcome. Take this deal, for example:

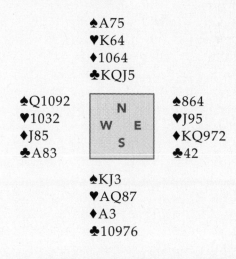

```
                  ♠A75
                  ♥K64
                  ♦1064
                  ♣KQJ5
  ♠Q1092                        ♠864
  ♥1032          N              ♥J95
  ♦J85        W     E           ♦KQ972
  ♣A83           S              ♣42
                  ♠KJ3
                  ♥AQ87
                  ♦A3
                  ♣10976
```

Now look at the difference in the auctions and the results between two pairs, the first using 12–14 no-trumps, the second 15–17 no-trumps. South is the dealer.

W	N	E	S
			1♣
P	3NT	P	P
P			

North's 3NT shows 13–15 HCP and indicates balanced shape without a four-card major. East will certainly lead his best suit—diamonds—and 3NT cannot be made legitimately. The ♦A can be held up only once. Although the heart suit splits favorably, providing four tricks, declarer has no choice but to go after clubs. As soon as he plays that suit, West will win the ace and play a diamond to his partner's hand. That's down one.

Now look what happens when South opens a 12–14 no-trump.

W	N	E	S
			1NT
P	3NT	P	P
P			

A player who sails into 3NT as North did rarely has a four-card major, so West will make his normal lead of a spade, presenting declarer with an extra trick in that suit but, more importantly, giving declarer time to knock out the ♣A and scamper home with two overtricks.

Obviously, this bonanza for North-South could have worked the other way. If the East-West hands were switched, the 1NT opener by South would have produced a minus score where most other North-South pairs were making game.

The point is that if you are willing to risk the poor scores produced by anti-field positions, there is a lot to be gained from being different.

♣ ♦ ♥ ♠

You don't have to be the same as everyone else to be happy or successful.

▶ Principle 27: Know the conventions for major-suit openings— and when to be unconventional.

In North America, if a player opens 1♥or 1♠, you can just about take it to the bank that the opening is based on a holding of at least five cards in the suit opened. Although most of the bridge teaching on this continent in the early days of contract bridge was based on four-card majors, the adherents of this system are just a small minority today. This is in contrast to the British, whose Acol system is based on 12–14 1NT openers and four-card majors.

The change to five-card majors has its genesis in the 1950s, when Alvin Roth, one of the great bidding theorists in the annals of bridge, teamed up with Tobias Stone to create a system employing five-card major openings.

All in all, five-card majors is a system that is fairly easy to play, and few if any of the thousands of bridge teachers out there are indoctrinating their students in alternative approaches. That means that you can sit down at the table with a new partner and know that you are likely to be playing the same basic system, with a few wrinkles here and there.

Does this mean that you should forget about ever playing four-card majors? Employing this system is another way to be anti-field, which can produce some outstanding results if things are going your way. Your primary concern in considering a move like this would be finding someone willing to go that way with you.

♣ ♦ ♥ ♠

Conventional wisdom may be valid for most, but the rewards reaped by free spirits and independent thinkers can be great and immensely satisfying.

▷ Principle 28: Beware of the Rule of 20.

Bridge players like to put things into easily remembered "rules." Some are nearly indispensable—to wit, the Rule of 11, which you apply to the opening lead of a spot card, especially against no-trump contracts. The Rule of 11 properly applied, can tell you a lot about the holdings of the opponents.

Another useful tool is the Rule of 8, which states that when your right-hand opponent opens with a weak two-bid and you are considering making a bid, it is logical to play partner for holding on average about 8 high-card points. He won't always have that much—and sometimes he will have more. It is a rough guideline aimed at enabling you to compete more comfortably.

Another "rule" that has gained favor in recent times is the Rule of 20, a guideline for helping you determine whether you should open the bidding. It has some validity, but if you blindly adhere to this "rule," you will be asking for trouble.

The rule is this: add up your high-card points and the number of cards in the two longest suits in your hand. If the number is 20 or higher, open with an appropriate suit bid.

In a general sense, the rule works, but you must also apply common sense and judgment to avoid trouble. Have a look at this hand:

♠AJ1098   ♥AJ873   ♦72   ♣9

You have 10 HCP and ten cards in your two longest suits. That's 20, so bid 'em up. The thing is, you don't need the Rule of 20 to tell you that this hand is a good opener. You have two good suits, increasing the chances that you have a fit with partner. If you can find partner with four or more in either major, you will take a lot of tricks. Also consider that your two long suits are headed by aces, and you should never underestimate how important that can be. It would not be a good idea to open the bidding if your hand looked like the following:

♠KQ754   ♥KQ432   ♦72   ♣9

It's 10 points, all right, and you have ten cards in your two long suits, but without the aces, the hands are not nearly as potent. If you found an eight-card fit in one of the suits and partner was also without the ace of the suit, the opponents, rather than you, would have a large measure of control. This hand should be passed.

♣ ♦ ♥ ♠

Rules and guidelines serve a valuable purpose,
but you should also think for yourself.

➤ Principle 29: Make adjustments to open in third seat.
If you decide to play sound opening bids, it will be necessary for you to make some adjustments. As strange as it may sound in the context of solid opening bids, you must open pretty light in third seat.

The reason you must do so has a lot to do with the concept of a particular deal belonging to one side or the other. That statement, "It's our hand," normally means that your side has the preponderance of the high-card points. Now if you are opening only "sound" hands in first and second seats, that means you will be passing some 12-point hands, even some 13-point hands on occasion. Does the idea of passing a 13-point hand make you a bit queasy? How about this one:

♠QJ   ♥KJ32   ♦QJ4   ♣QJ32

That's 13 HCP, all right, but it's about as lousy a 13 points as you will see. Flat shape, three sets of "quacks," and a moth-eaten heart suit with pitiful spots. Opening this hand could get you in a lot of trouble. If you and partner are in tune on third-seat openers, however, you will pass this one without a care.

As a brief aside, it's important not to study too long before passing if you choose to do so. There's a concept in bridge called the "12-point hitch." What it means is that, if you study more than is normal, then pass, everyone knows you probably have close to an opening hand. This information is not authorized for your partner, but it's fair game for the opponents. Try very hard to avoid those telltale hitches.

Back to the third-seat question. The reason you must keep the bidding open with some 10- and 11-point hands—even an occasional 9—is that it can be a disaster for your side to pass out a deal when you have 23 or 24 HCP between you. Even with two bad hands facing each other, you are due a plus score if you have that many HCP. If you pass and the next player cannot keep the bidding open—or chooses not to—you will pay dearly.

There is another important concept to keep in mind regarding third-seat openers. Because you will be opening light on occasion, you must not take another bid with a substandard hand. If you open 1♣ in third seat, the next player passes, and partner bids something, if you do anything but pass, you are guaranteeing a full opening bid.

With that in mind, here are some hands you would want to bid with in third seat as insurance against partner's having passed a 12- or 13-point hand.

♠KQ4	♥A1076	♦Q1043	♣109
♠QJ43	♥KJ76	♦QJ2	♣109
♠AJ76	♥A1098	♦1098	♣109

If you open 1♦ on any of these, you will be in a position to pass any response partner makes, be it a major suit, 1NT—even 2♣, which should be based on a five-card suit.

An even better plan would be to agree with partner that an opening bid of a major suit in third seat might be made on a four-card suit.

There is a very important caveat about light third-seat openers: do not open if your hand is not suitable for a pass of any bid that partner might make.

♣ ♦ ♥ ♠

You will be better off if you always keep in mind
where you are and make adjustments accordingly.

> **Principle 30: Understand what it means to open in fourth seat.**

In opening light in third seat, you are in a very real sense "protecting" partner against having made a good decision to pass a poorly constructed 12- or 13-point hand. When the bidding comes to you in fourth seat—your left-hand opponent was dealer and there have been three passes to you—it is a different matter entirely. You may actually end up passing some pretty good hands—and your two-level openings will be anything but weak bids.

The determining factor in your decision to open at the one level may surprise you. It's not high cards, spot cards, or quick tricks. It's the spade suit. Say you are sitting in fourth seat and there have been three passes to you, and your hand is

♠J2   ♥AK1098   ♦K10   ♣8654

You have a nice heart suit, two-and-a-half quick tricks—and no way to keep the opponents from outbidding you if they have a spade fit. If you pass, you will get no score. You might have a plus on this deal if you open and find that partner has passed a decent hand in second seat.

There is the very real chance, however, that the high-card points are pretty evenly distributed around the table, and if the opponents possess the spade suit, they will outbid you. The last thing you want to hear if you open 1♥ is a 1♠ bid from the player who passed in first seat. Your partner might be able to raise your hearts, but if the player in third seat can raise *his* partner . . . well, your decision to bid will turn a no score into a minus.

There is a good rule of thumb for deciding whether to open in fourth seat. It's called the Rule of 15, or Cansino Count in some circles. The rule is this: add up your high-card points and the number of spades you hold. If the number is 15 or higher, go ahead and open. If it's less, fold 'em up and move on to the next deal. Interestingly, the late Rixi Markus, a world champion and one of Great Britain's greatest players, believed that the Rule of 15 was valid in most cases, but she made an exception when she held a singleton or a void in spades. Her thinking was that extreme shortness in spades made it more likely that her partner held length in the suit.

♣ ♦ ♥ ♠

You will do better in any undertaking if you
study the subject and learn its subtleties.

▷ **Principle 31: Know the difference between tricks and high-card points.**

It's great to have lots of high-card points. It's better to have lots of tricks, and tricks come in the form of trumps. Taken in the extreme, a hand with thirteen cards of one suit has only 10 HCP—the ace, king, queen, and jack of the suit—but it has thirteen tricks. You won't see that hand, of course, if you play for 100 years (unless someone is having some fun with you). You will see, however, lots of eight-card suits, an occasional nine and even a ten-card suit. There was a bridge player, now deceased, who lived in Memphis. On the two occasions when she was dealt ten-card suits, her partner passed out of turn. According to the rules of the game, she was barred from the bidding. Imagine being dealt ten-card suits twice and not getting to bid either time!

The annals of bridge are filled with tales of players who overcalled on high-card points, got doubled, and went down so much the score looked like a telephone number. It seems the lament is always, "But partner, I had 15 points!" What he needed was tricks.

Say your right-hand opponent opens 1♠ and your hand is as follows:

♠Q63   ♥AK832   ♦K7   ♣Q72

That's 14 HCP—and a disaster waiting to happen. Consider that your right-hand opponent probably has about 13 HCP. With your 15, that's 28. That means partner and your left-hand opponent have 12 HCP to divide between them. If it comes out even, partner will have about 6 HCP. You won't like it if partner's hand is something like the following:

♠J1064   ♥J   ♦QJ43   ♣8654

That's pretty close to what you could expect in terms of HCP, but you will probably be doubled if you bid—and you will go down a lot. Your left-hand opponent is short in spades, and your opponents have seven hearts to your five and partner's one.

Now change the hand somewhat.

♠53   ♥AKJ1097   ♦K1098   ♣5

It's "only" 11 HCP, but your heart suit will take at least five tricks opposite a void. Your second suit is chunky. This hand has lots of potential tricks, whereas the other version could well take only three or four tricks.

When it comes to overcalling at the two level, forget about the points. It's tricks you want to count.

♣ ♦ ♥ ♠

Sometimes it is hard to see what's important and truly valuable.
Take time to look beneath the surface.

Chapter 5

Talking Back to Partner—
Keeping the Conversation Going

The conversation that you have with your partner in the bidding can be very delicate at times. It's important to stay within the parameters of the bidding system you have agreed upon. If you violate your agreements, you are sowing the seeds of destruction for your partnership. Keep faith with partner and he will keep faith with you.

➤ Principle 32: Don't "rescue" partner with a bad hand after a minor-suit opener.
When you play five-card major openings, sometimes you have to open one of a minor on a very bad holding. The following deal is a good example:

♠AJ109   ♥QJ43   ♦AQ   ♣432

It's only 14 high-card points, so you can't open 1NT. You don't have five of a major, so 1♥or 1♠ is out, although some players would open 1♥ anyway, especially if the cards in the majors were switched. Most players, however, would stick to the system and open 1♣, although they would hate doing it.

One of the all-time great bridge raconteurs, the late Ron Andersen, loved to tell the story about his mother's bridge club. When the ladies played, Andersen often related, the opening bid with the example hand would be "a club." If the suit was a bit more robust, the opening bid would be a straightforward "one club." When the suit was long *and* strong, opener offered, "I'll start with a club."

Andersen's story, although entertaining, was no doubt apocryphal—and relaying information in that way is strictly forbidden by the proprieties of bridge. Therefore, in real life, when partner opens 1♣, you can't tell whether partner has a fistful of very good clubs, or three little bitty ones.

The possibility that it's the weaker holding generates a sense of panic in some players, so much so that they abandon reason and common sense and make bids they have no business even thinking about.

Does this mean you should never bid over partner's minor-suit opening with a really bad hand? No, but you must pick your spots, and it helps if you are playing the convention known as the weak jump shift.

♣ ♦ ♥ ♠

Sometimes it's just best to grin and bear it
and let an unpleasant situation run its course.

▷ Principle 33: A 1♦ opener is likely to be at least four cards in length.

There is but one occasion when it is necessary to open 1♦ on a three-card suit: when your hand pattern is 4-4-3-2, with specifically four cards in each major, three cards in diamonds, and two in clubs. Otherwise, your opening bid of 1♦ will show at least four cards. You will open 1♣ on a three-card suit much more often—with the hand pattern just given, with 4-3-3-3 when you have three cards in each minor and with 4-4-2-3.

Knowing that 1♦ is most often at least four cards will help you with those feelings of panic when you have a poor hand and a poor holding in diamonds. You won't feel as nervous passing, which is your best move in the long run.

♣ ♦ ♥ ♠

A good grasp of technical knowledge can give
you confidence in approaching a task.

➤ Principle 34: Obey the captain.

There is a very important principle in bridge that might sound more like a rule for the high seas. It's about captaincy.

Once the partnership starts the conversation that is the auction, one of the partners should strive to limit his hand as soon as possible. If someone doesn't do that, the auction will not progress as smoothly.

There are many bids that limit one's hand. A 1NT opener, for example, describes a hand with a narrow limit, usually 15–17 HCP. When opener starts with one of a minor and rebids 1NT over partner's major-suit response, that bid limits the hand to 14 HCP. With more, the opener would have been 1NT—or the rebid might have been 2NT (18 or 19 HCP).

When opener begins with one of a minor and responder bids 1NT, that usually shows 6–9 or 8–10 HCP (depending on the partnership agreement), and it also indicates that responder does not have a four-card major.

As soon as one member of the partnership limits his hand, the other member of the partnership is captain. The captain now knows approximately how high the two hands should go in the bidding. The captain looks at his own hand and combines it with the maximum partner can have, then settles for a part score, bids a games or makes an invitation. The captain's partner is bound by the captain's decision.

In general, opener will limit his hand with his first rebid. If responder limits his hand first, however, opener becomes captain.

♣ ♦ ♥ ♠

Personal goals and a team effort are not mutually exclusive pursuits, and you will be more successful if you are seen as a team player.

▷ Principle 35: "Bashing" is often better than "science."

For some people, there's nothing better than a laborious, intricate auction to just the right spot. Some bidding systems are so precise that partners can identify jacks in each other's hands. The auction might go on forever, but the players can arrive at just the right spot when unimpeded.

The trouble is, every bit of information exchanged between the two bidders is also available to the opponents. That's the way bridge works. You are not allowed to have a secret bidding system with your partner. You must disclose your bidding agreements to the opponents whenever they ask for information. If you and your partner have taken fourteen bids to arrive at your final contract, the opponent on lead is entitled to ask the meaning of each bid you made.

This can have a devastating effect on your success in the contract you have arrived at so carefully. You are much better off in many cases by simply blasting to the contract you have in mind, leaving it to the opening leader to figure out what to do.

Consider your position as South on the following deal:

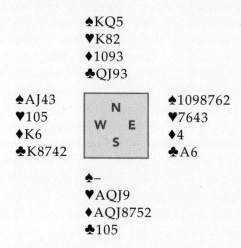

Which of the following two auctions do you like best?

W	N	E	S
			1♦
P	2NT	P	6♦
All Pass			

W	N	E	S
			1♦
P	2NT	P	3♥
P	3♠	P	4♦
P	5♦	All Pass	

Your rationale for simply leaping to 6♦ is this: Your partner has denied a four-card major with his bid of 2NT (11–12 HCP), meaning he will almost certainly have diamond support for you. He is also likely to have high cards in clubs that could help you out. Further, he tends to have stoppers in at least one of the majors, so the ♥K is not out of the question. That gives you a great chance for twelve tricks with your great-looking hand. You might even make thirteen.

In the first auction, West would have to guess what to lead. Many players holding the West hand—looking at a virtually certain trick with the ♦K behind the opening bidder—would start with the ♠A, with disastrous results. South ruffs the ♠A, goes to dummy with the ♥K, and pitches his two losing clubs on the two high spades. He loses the diamond finesse to the king, but his slam is home.

Despite the result, the ♠A could well be the correct lead if the North had the ♠Q105 and the ♣AQ93 and South was holding two low spades and a void in clubs. A club lead would give South a free finesse and allow him to pitch away his two losing spades.

The point is that West does not have a lot of information to steer him to the killing opening lead.

Contrast this with the second auction, where South opts to describe his hand more accurately for partner—and for the opponents. The 3♥ bid can only be a slam try, and North cooperates by showing his values in spades. Now, without a club control, South must mark time with a bid of 4♦. He would like to bid 4♣, but he has neither first- nor second-round control in clubs. South hopes North can cuebid clubs, but North is similarly stymied in that department and can do no more than sign off in game.

Well, guess what? Unless West is deaf or trying very hard to curry favor with South, he will put a club on the track as fast he can get it out of his hand. North and South have pinpointed the opening lead and now South, with an excellent shot at slam if he simply bashed into it, will go down in *game*!

Sailing into slam this way is not recommended as a regular diet. There will, of course, be occasions when West will be dealt both of the high clubs—and he'll probably defeat your slam even if you bash into it rather than giving information with slam tries and cuebids.

The point is that it is often right to forget about scientific auctions that give up too much information and simply bid what you think you can make. Very often, your estimate will turn out to be accurate.

♣ ♦ ♥ ♠

*It is rarely a good strategy to immediately expose
your strong points to your opposition.*

➤ Principle 36: Don't bid the same values twice.
This is a corollary to the captaincy principle. There are many ways to violate that covenant with your partner. Here are just a couple of examples.

Suppose your hand is the following:

♠65   ♥AJ   ♦KJ10654   ♣QJ9

This is a reasonable if not robust opening bid, so you start with 1♦. The next player passes and partner bids 1♥. Now your right-hand opponent gums up the works with a bid of 2♠. It's your move.

It seems natural to bid 3♦. You have a six-card suit that so far has not been described, so you want to get in there and bid it. Don't.

If you bid freely at the three level, you are showing much more strength than you have. Your opener is a bare minimum, the six-card suit notwithstanding, and a disciplined pass tells that story.

Don't forget, partner's hand is unlimited, and he is sitting at the table, too. If he has the right hand, he will do something over 2♠, possibly a so-called balancing double (assuming that your left-hand opponent passes after you do). If partner is very weak, he will pass and you will have escaped a bidding "accident" that didn't need to happen.

Here's another common situation. You hold the following hand.

♠J98   ♥AKJ2   ♦9876   ♣84

You are sitting South and participate in the following auction. Both sides are vulnerable.

W	N	E	S
1♣	1♠	2♣	2♠
3♣	P	P	?

If you have never heard of the principle under discussion, you might consider bidding 3♠ here. Big mistake. Partner heard you bid 2♠. He knows that you might have a hand as good as the one you're looking at, yet he chose to pass over 3♣. It is an egregious error to bid 3♠ in this situation, especially vulnerable. Yes, partner might luck out and make it, or go down only one when the opponents can make 110 or 130 in a club part score, but partner will be just as likely to go minus 200—a very bad score if you are playing in a duplicate game—and the opponents still have the option of doubling. Then a one-trick set will produce the same dreadful minus 200.

*It is important to be disciplined as a team member
and to keep group goals in mind as you make decisions.*

➤ Principle 37: Have fun with two over one.
Most modern players—certainly those who play duplicate—are at least familiar with the bidding system known as 2/1 Game Force.

The cornerstone of this system is the principle that a two-level response to an opening bid is forcing to game. To wit: 1♠ by you, 2♣ by your partner. You are not allowed to stop bidding until you have reached some game contract. The notable exception is when the opening and responding hands are complete misfits—that is, you are short in partner's suits, and vice versa.

Most of the time, however, when someone makes a two-level response to an opening bid, you're getting to some game.

The advantage to this system is that you and partner don't have to go jumping around, using valuable bidding space, to describe your hands to each other.

Just so you understand, 2/1 Game Force is not a foolproof system. It does have flaws, and it is more complicated than Standard, which can tax the memory. In the main, however, it is the system favored by most tournament players.

Don't scoff at the newest innovations if you haven't tried them.

Chapter 6

To Pass or Not to Pass

There is nothing more frustrating for a player than to make a bid, expecting a response from partner, only to hear a pass. Anyone who has played bridge for any length of time has had the experience and can attest to the anxiety created when a "forcing" bid is passed. Of course, these episodes do make for some good stories—like playing a five-level spade contract with three trumps between the two hands. These can be funny anecdotes, as long as you don't have too many of them.

> ▷ **Principle 38: Know what's forcing and what isn't.**

You probably learned long ago in your bridge education that any new suit by an unpassed hand in response to an opening bid cannot be passed. It is, in the vernacular, forcing. The only excuse you would have for not bidding again would be if you had made a psychic opening bid (don't do it—more on that later) or if you were stricken with a heart attack in mid-auction and rushed to the hospital. Even then, partner might show up in your room and expect you to continue the auction.

  Thus, if you open 1♣ and partner responds 1♥, you are not allowed to pass. It's true that 1♥ does not sound like a lot, but that bid does not limit the responder's hand in any way. If you and your partner are using strong jump-shift responses, you can rule out a very strong hand with a long, strong heart suit, but just about anything else is possible.

That situation, of course, is easy. There are many other situations in which you are expected to bid in response to your partner's bid. Here are a few.

1. If partner bids 4NT, asking for aces, you must answer his question.

2. If you and your partner have voluntarily bid a game and the opponents have sacrificed, you or your partner may pass to give the other the option of bidding on or doubling. The one action you may not take is passing. Thus, if your partner says pass in that situation, it is a "forcing pass." You can double or bid—but not pass.

3. If you bid a suit bid by one of the opponents—known as a cuebid—your partner is not allowed to pass. It is not an offer to play there. The cuebid is meant to show extra strength and/or a control in that suit (the ace, the king, a singleton, or a void). The annals of bridge are replete with stories of passed cuebids. You can be certain that it's not fun to play 5♠ when you hold the singleton ace of that suit opposite three to the 6.

4. If you and your partner are bidding along (as the opponents pass) and one of you bids the fourth suit, as in 1♣–1♥; 1♠–2♦, that is a bid that cannot be passed. Most players agree that if a member of a partnership employs "fourth-suit forcing," it is forcing to game. You may not pass until some game contract is reached.

These are some of the many situations that are considered forcing. It's a good idea to discuss them with your partner to make sure there are no "accidents."

♣ ♦ ♥ ♠

Be sure you understand what your colleagues are saying.

➤ Principle 39: Learn to pass.

As you gain experience, you will have a greater understanding of the temptations that the game can place before you. Where the auction is concerned, most of those temptations will be to overbid or to make some other rash decision that will come back to haunt you.

Let's say you are playing in a duplicate game and you hold the following hand:

♠10   ♥8   ♦AQJ107643   ♣762

Let's say the opponents are vulnerable and you are not, and you decide to open 4♦, a bid that shows lots and lots of diamonds—typically eight of them—and an otherwise weak hand.

Your left-hand opponent passes, as does partner, and now your right-hand opponent chirps, "Four hearts."

Now you are regretting that you didn't bid 5♦ to start with. You rationalize that it's not too late. You can still bid it. After all, if they make 4♥ they'll score 620. You are not vulnerable and you have that great diamond suit. How bad could it be to bid 5♦?

It could be very bad. The following might be the entire deal:

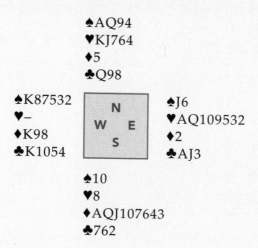

♠AQ94
♥KJ764
♦5
♣Q98

♠K87532   ♠J6
♥—   ♥AQ109532
♦K98   ♦2
♣K1054   ♣AJ3

♠10
♥8
♦AQJ107643
♣762

You goaded East into making a dubious bid (although not completely insane), and partner was waiting with glee for his chance to double 4♥—but you kept him from doing it by bidding 5♦. West, of course, would double that contract—he couldn't double your first bid because it would not have been for penalty—and you would go down at least two tricks on a deal where you are probably going to get plus 500 or 800 in 4♥ doubled.

This is just one example of temptation, and an extreme one at that. There will be other temptations that are much more subtle. You must train yourself to resist them.

Pass is probably the most underutilized weapon in your arsenal. When you learn to wield it properly, it can be devastating.

♣ ♦ ♥ ♠

Sometimes in life the most productive action you can take is none at all.

➤ Principle 40: Cut the auction short when a misfit is discovered.

You have been taught that when your partner opens the bidding and you have an opening hand yourself, you should not stop bidding until you reach some game. Every now and then, that will not be possible. Most of the time when you stop short, it will be because your hand and your partner's do not fit at all.

There have been many auctions like the following one, especially between two less-experienced players.

W	N	E	S
P	1♠	P	2♣
P	2♠	P	3♣
P	3♥	P	4♣
P	4♠	Dbl	5♣
Dbl	All Pass		

Down 800, maybe more. North probably has a singleton or void in clubs, South the same in spades. Neither has anything in diamonds, or someone might have tried no-trump. All the signs were there. The auction should have stopped at 3♣. At a certain point in an auction like this—with the partnership fighting it out—the opponents smell blood, and they are usually quick to pounce. Of course, when the hands fit so badly, there is no place to run once they start doubling.

♣ ♦ ♥ ♠

When you find yourself in a situation where you clash with another person, it's often best to simply back away.

➤ Principle 41: Avoid nullo bids.

A nullo bid is one that has a high likelihood of losing and rarely wins even if luck is on your side. An extreme example might be bidding 6♠ when vulnerable as a sacrifice against a nonvulnerable

6♥, hoping that (1) the contract will go down less than the value of their slam or (2) that they will bid on to 7♥ and perhaps go down.

In a duplicate game, such an action would be lunacy. For starters, 6♥ might not be making. Second, in a typical pair game slams are not bid that often, so your sacrifice (minus score) will actually be compared to a lot of game scores. That means that even if 6♥ is cold and you somehow manage to go down only 500 or 800, that score will not compare favorably to all the 480s around the room. Third, you could go down considerably more than the slam score. Fourth, and worst of all, you might push them into a grand slam that can't be defeated, so even if lots of pairs are bidding the small slam, you just gave yourself a zero by pushing them into 7♥.

In a more mundane setting, it's usually poor practice to balance at the three level when vulnerable. Consider the following hand:

♠Q5   ♥J543   ♦A6   ♣Q6543

You are South. Your side is vulnerable and you hear the following auction:

W	N	E	S
		1♠	P
2♠	P	P	?

It is usually right to try to boost the level of the opponents' bidding with a tactic called "balancing." When the auction has ended at a low level as above, you can draw the inference that partner has some assets. If the opponents had more between them, they probably would have made a mild stab at game. The abrupt halt to the bidding means partner has something over there. You might also call on the well-worn principle that if their side has a fit, the odds favor your side having a fit as well.

Even so, you must go quietly here. Bidding 3♣ in this situation is a nullo bid. The opponents have exchanged information about their hands. They will know what they can make and what they can't, and they won't let you push them around. They need only five tricks against you in a doubled contract to earn a good score (plus 200).

There is a famous deal from a world championship in the 1990s when a Swedish player, holding ♦J1098, doubled his opponents in 7♦. They promptly ran to 7NT, which could not be defeated. Had the player with the sure diamond trick just kept his mouth shut, he had a guaranteed plus score. Thanks to his nullo decision to double, he traded plus 50 for minus 1520.

♣ ♦ ♥ ♠

Your self-esteem will increase if you work to avoid silly errors.

▷ Principle 42: Being predictable is not necessarily bad.

No one wants to be thought of as ho-hum or predictable. You want your opponents to respect your creativity. You want to put pressure on them through aggressive bidding. There are situations, however, where you should always do the same thing rather than guessing what to do.

A common situation would be when an opponent bids after partner has opened 1NT. You may choose to be aggressive or conservative, but stick to one or the other. Don't try to guess which way to go with similar hands. You could, in theory, guess wrong every time and go on a losing streak that lasts for months.

If you take the same action every time, you will be right some of the time, with an advantage if you choose to be aggressive. Consider the following hand.

♠4   ♥AJ1098   ♦7643   ♣QJ9

Your partner opens 1NT and the next player bids 2♠. If you bid 3♥, it is forcing to game. You don't have a way to invite game—and you certainly can't double with a singleton spade. If you pass, 2♠ will likely be the final contract. It's your choice. What you must not do is pass with this hand some of the time and bid with it on other occasions. You either bid or pass.

Here is why you should err on the side of aggression. First, if you commit your side to game, it may be an unbeatable contract (you will end up in 4♥ or 3NT). Second, even if you don't have the assets for game, the opponents don't know that, and they may take a sacrifice against your final contract when they were booked for a plus just by passing. In the vernacular, such a move is known as a "phantom" sacrifice—saving against a game that wasn't making. Third, just because you are supposed to go down doesn't mean you will. For many players, defense is the toughest part of the game. They may let you make it.

In actuality, doing the same thing every time on hands such as this is not really being predictable. The opponents don't know, of course, whether you were pushing a bit or if you have pulled in your horns. On the other hand, if you pass 2♠ around to partner and he knows your aggressive tendencies, he won't feel anxious about passing himself. He will be sure, at least, that you're not losing out on a game.

♣ ♦ ♥ ♠

A team needs members who are steady.
You enhance your standing when others can count on you consistently.

➤ Principle 43: Expect interference.

In the old days of bridge, if someone opened the bidding, he and his partner pretty much had the auction all to themselves. This was especially true if the opening bid was 1NT. In the early days of contract bridge, 1NT showed a balanced hand with 16 to 18 high-card points. You entered the auction at your peril, or so most players thought.

Nowadays, players are taught from their bridge "infancy" that they should get in there and compete. More and more players are becoming familiar with the law of total tricks, which emphasizes the number of trumps more than high-card points. In other words, having 10 spades between two hands will make up for a lot of missing aces, kings, and queens.

You can read more about the law of total tricks later in this book. For now, it's in your best interest to understand that you rarely will have a free run in the auction—nor should you fail to get in there and bid yourself.

This doesn't mean that you should bid with anything—and you can very easily get yourself into trouble with reckless bidding—but the requirements for competing are not what they once were. In the old days, many players believed that an overcall showed the equivalent of an opening hand. That's why so many auctions went smoothly for the opening side. Today's players need little more than a decent suit to get into the bidding. Take a look at the following hand:

♠AKJ105   ♥J4   ♦10987   ♣63

If your right-hand opponent opened at the one level (1♣, 1♦, or 1♥), any red-blooded duplicate player would be right there with a bid of 1♠. It's "only" 9 HCP, but not much bad could happen to you in 1♠—and if you happen to go down, they can probably make something better. If you know that bidding with that hand is correct, your opponents will, too—and they'll be in there just as you would.

There are no easy rides. You have to fight for what's yours.

♣ ♦ ♥ ♠

Nothing worth achieving is easy.

> **Principle 44: Make sure you know how to handle interference.**

There is another factor in today's game that has created more of a tendency to interfere with the opponents' auctions. It's the super-light opening bids you see more and more often. If your opponents are opening all kinds of trashy hands, and you let this keep you out of the bidding, they'll steal you blind. Once you get into the habit of competing, it's kind of addictive. You will not be successful every time you enter their auctions, but you will be a winner in the long run if you bid 'em up.

That said, you better be prepared for the opponents to do the same. At a minimum, you must add negative doubles to your arsenal. It is not within the scope of this book to teach you negative doubles. If you don't play this convention, however, you will be at a severe disadvantage in the normal tournament crowd.

There are other conventions devised to handle all the interference you will encounter as the opponents become more and more aggressive. Make it your business to learn them.

♣ ♦ ♥ ♠

It's important to take the right tools to the job.

Chapter 7

It's a Bidder's Game

Just as it's important to seize the initiative and open the bidding whenever it's reasonable to do so, it's also key to your success to be active. If you never overcall unless you have the Rock of Gibraltar for a hand, you will be easy to play against. If you are afraid to go down and bid accordingly, you will be giving the opponents a free ticket to their best contract nearly every time. That's not the path to success.

> **Principle 45: Busy bidders are tough opponents.**
There's a difference between "busy" and "crazy." Make it your goal to learn the difference.

When the opponents open the bidding, they have fired the first shot. They have the advantage. If you don't get in there and mix it up, they will certainly land in the right spot. Modern bidding has progressed to the point that when opponents are unimpeded in the bidding, they will almost always stop on the proverbial dime.

If you and your partner are in there bidding your own suits and taking up their bidding space, the opponents' bidding becomes much less precise.

Don't be afraid of bad results. If you are an aggressive, busy bidder, you will get too high now and then, the opponents will double and you will get a very bad score. Look at it this way: If you get above-average or excellent scores three times for every time you get nailed, you are still way ahead of the game.

That's not to say you should bid regardless of your holdings. If you become a crazy bidder, you will lose your partner's confidence and your partnership will flounder.

Wild is not necessary. Aggressive will do just fine.

♣ ♦ ♥ ♠

You can't forge ahead if you are unwilling to move.

➤ Principle 46: Four-card overcalls can be deadly.

This may go against the grain for some players, but there is a lot to be gained from overcalling on four-card suits. Just be sure to pick your spots—and make sure your spots have been picked well. That's another way of saying that you shouldn't overcall with ratty four-card suits. A minimum would be something like AJ98. Remember, too, that the context of the auction and the overall makeup of your hand will factor into your decision about overcalling with a four-card suit.

♠AJ109   ♥Q42   ♦J543   ♣109

If your right-hand opponent opens one of a minor, a 1♠ over-call would not be out of line. The effect of the bid can be telling, particularly if the opponents do not have an eight-card fit in hearts. Neither may have a stopper in spades, so they will be reluctant to bid no-trump—and they may miss the best game as a result. They don't know, after all, that your side can take only four spade tricks. You might also find partner with a shapely hand and a great spade fit, in which case you may be able to blow them out of the water with preemptive action.

A four-card overcall can also be a great lead directing bid, particularly when your four-card suit is headed by the AKQ. If partner ends up on lead and you didn't give him a hint about the opening lead, chances are he won't find your suit. After all, he can't have more than a jack.

There is less of an incentive to overcall with a four-card spade suit when the opening bid was 1♥. If the opponents have an eight-card or better heart fit, they won't have any trouble finding it. You might still overcall for lead direction, but overall hand quality is more of a concern—and be very careful when you are vulnerable.

Be aware that this strategy can backfire on occasion—especially when your overcall steers the opponents away from playing in a suit they would have chosen had you not intervened. If you have only four of them, the opponents could well have an eight- or even a nine-card fit in that suit. Bidding it, particularly in the case of majors, will keep them from picking that suit for trumps.

♣ ♦ ♥ ♠

It's comfortable to conform, but it can be stifling.

> **Principle 47: Take your best shot right away. Don't back in.**
There's a tired old strategy in bridge called "walking the dog." It's basically this: You have a good hand and a long, strong suit. The auction is competitive. Rather than just blasting to the contract you know you can make, you take it slow and easy, hoping that somewhere along the way the opponents will double you, resulting in a big score for your side.

That works in some settings, but if you give the opponents extra bidding room, they will be able to exchange information and will be in a better position to judge what to do if you wait to take the action you knew you were going to take all along.

♠4　　♥AQJ98　　♦5432　　♣943

Your partner opens 3♥ and the next player doubles for takeout. Why mess around? You can be certain that you are taking no heart tricks—one of the opponents must be void—and partner is supposed to have a weak hand with long hearts. Bid 6♥ straightaway. Don't give someone a chance to cuebid to show first-round control of the suit.

Here's another situation.

♠J7654   ♥5   ♦K1098   ♣J43

Your left-hand opponent opens 1♣ and partner bids 2♣, a convention bid showing at least five cards in each major. Whatever the next player does, your bid should be 4♠. If your partner had overcalled 1♠, you would certainly raise him to four with your hand. Don't give the opponents room to maneuver. Put it to them right away.

♣ ♦ ♥ ♠

You can choose to be timid or bold.
Project confidence and you will have more success.

➤ **Principle 48: Get to know the law of total tricks.**
The theory surrounding the law of total tricks was first expounded in the 1950s by a Frenchman, who postulated that on most deals, the number of tricks available was equal to the total of the cards the two sides held in their best fits. In other words, if North-South hold nine spades between them, while East-West hold ten hearts, there should be a total of nineteen tricks, give or take a trick or two. This is a gross oversimplification, to be sure, and there are many exceptions, but in general it is a useful guideline.

The Law, as proponents like to call it, has had a profound effect on modern bidding, thanks to Larry Cohen and Marty Bergen. These two former partners based their very aggressive bidding system on The Law and the protection that really good trump fits provide when the bidding heats up.

Cohen went one step further and wrote a book on the sub-ject—possibly the most influential bridge book of the twentieth century. Today, you encounter more and more players jumping around in the bidding and putting pressure on their opponents, feeling the safety of 9- and 10-card trump fits. Bidding systems are geared to uncover such fits, to the chagrin of their opponents.

If you don't know much about the law of total tricks, make it your business to find out more.

♣ ♦ ♥ ♠

Innovative thinking is the cornerstone of progress.

➤ Principle 49: Don't be afraid to live on the edge.
This is an especially important principle for those who choose to play duplicate, the most interesting and exciting form of contract bridge.

Since your scores in duplicate come from comparisons rather than from the total score at the table, you are more aware of what others might do with the hands you hold. You want to distinguish yourself from them in any way possible. A mere overtrick in your contract can make the difference between an average score and a great score—a "top" in the vernacular of duplicate. One way to distinguish yourself from your opponents is to take more tricks than they do. If you are a skilled declarer, you may well reap the rewards of your expertise.

Another way to earn those comparison bonuses is to engineer smaller minuses than the other players who are holding the same hands you hold. For example, if the opponents have bid to 2♠ and can make it, your score will be minus 110 (in duplicate, you get your trick scores plus 50 points for making your contract). If you can buy the contract at 3♣, however, and you go down one, that's only minus 50 (assuming you are not vulnerable). Since you get a point for every pair you outscore, that minus 50 can be big if all the other pairs have recorded minus 110. Even if the opponents double you and you go down, that's only minus 100—still better than minus 110.

That's a simplified example of how you work to find any advantage possible. It's also why you take chances in duplicate you might not take in rubber bridge and why, when your side finds a great trump fit, you are willing to bid 'em up to put pressure on the opponents. You don't want anything to be easy for them. After all, they're trying to make it hard on you, too.

♠J4   ♥Q987   ♦65   ♣AK654

You are sitting South. Neither side is vulnerable.

W	N	E	S
1♠	P	2♠	?

If you are thinking about bidding 3♣ here, you have the makings of a tough tournament player. There is definite risk involved in bidding with this hand. If your partner is broke, you could end up being doubled, going down a ton. Instead of that hoped-for "top," you might end up with the opposite—a "zero." Still, it's worth the risk. West might well be poised to blast into game, leaving your partner clueless about the opening lead. With your bid to guide him, he might find the only lead to hold declarer to ten tricks. If everyone else playing the East-West cards makes eleven or twelve tricks and you hold them to ten, you have achieved a fantastic score. Of course, if you are doubled and go down 800, you will have to pay off, but that's part of the adventure.

No one should take risks for the sake of doing so.
It's a good strategy, however, if the potential rewards are great.

> **Principle 50: Be familiar with the weapons at your disposal.**

There are many ways to be a busy bidder—to make life difficult for your opponents. It will pay you to know the elementary ones. Knowledge of these tools is the bare minimum for playing in tournaments. You don't have to use all the bids if you don't want to, but you will be completely lost if you don't even know what they are.

The takeout double, of course, is one of the most popular and efficient ways of getting into the bidding. That requires a certain strength of hand, however. Other ways of getting into the bidding don't necessarily require lots of high-card points.

Bids that show two suits at once are fan favorites: the Michaels cuebid and the Unusual No-trump.

A Michaels cuebid is used after an opponent opens the bidding at the one level. A bid of opener's suit—as in 1♣–2♣—is not an offer to play in clubs. By agreement, it shows both major suits. Most players require that each major be at least five cards long. The high-card strength is not so strict.

♠QJ987   ♥J10764   ♦4   ♣J3

This would be a reasonable Michaels bid after a 1♣ opener (assuming your side is not vulnerable).

♠QJ1098   ♥KJ1098   ♦32   ♣10

This would be even better. Both long suits have chunky spots and will provide tricks even if the other hand is short in both majors.

Michaels is not meant to show a very strong hand, but you can use it when you have a powerhouse and want only for partner to select a suit.

♠AKQ65   ♥KQJ104   ♦A   ♣65

If your right-hand opponent opens 1♣ or 1♦, you will bid two of the minor. When your partner selects a major, you will bid game in that suit—4♠ or 4♥—and consider your side unlucky if the contract goes down.

Michaels can be used when the opening bid is a major. Bidding two of the major that was opened shows a hand with five of the other major and at least five of an unspecified minor. If your partner doesn't like your major, he can bid 3♣, telling you to pass if that is your minor suit, or bid 3♦. Either way, he likes the minor better than your major.

The Unusual No-trump can be used over any bid as well. Over a major-suit opening, 2NT—an "unusual" bid because it normally shows great strength—shows at least 5-5 in the minor suits. Over a minor-suit opener, 2NT shows the two lowest unbid suits: hearts and diamonds over 1♣ and hearts and clubs over 1♦.

Even if you don't want to play these conventions, you must have knowledge of them because nearly all of your opponents will be wheeling them out against you every chance they get.

♣ ♦ ♥ ♠

The Boy Scouts have the right idea: Be prepared.

> **Principle 51: Take care with your preemptive bids.**

It's important to take up bidding space from the opponents whenever you can, and it might seem that players who are always jumping around in the bidding are wild and undisciplined. That may be true with some of them, but ones who know what they are doing follow strict rules.

The number-one rule to follow is to avoid making a weak bid (such as an opening bid of 3♦) with defensive tricks outside your suit. Preemptive bidding can pay off handsomely with sacrifices or "saves." For example, the vulnerable opponents can make plus 620 in 4♠, while 5♦ by you, even doubled, goes down only 500 (you are not vulnerable). The problem comes when your partner takes a sacrifice in your suit against their nonmaker, which is a nonmaker because you have an ace and/or a king outside your long suit.

This is fun for the opponents and very annoying to your partner.

The point is that when you start off at the three level in the bidding, you announce a weak hand with your assets concentrated in your long suit. If you continually make weak bids with defensive tricks outside your suit, your partner will never know whether it's right to save—and he will tend to give up on the practice after the second or third time he realizes another "phantom" save has been perpetrated, and you will miss out on a lot of profitable sacrifice bids.

You will earn the respect of others if your word is your bond.

Chapter 8

The Tools You Use—Conventions That Have Nothing to Do with Meetings

Charles Goren, the bridge guru whose heyday was in the 1940s and '50s, would not recognize the modern world of bridge bidding today. There are so many "gadgets" for bidding—also known as "conventions"—that it's impossible to know them all. A book on the subject by Amalya Kearse is more than 1,000 pages long. It's folly to try to put all of these bidding agreements into your bridge arsenal, but there are some very valuable conventions you don't want to leave home without.

➤ **Principle 52: First and foremost, use the best "tool" you own: your ears. Listen to the bidding.**

There are literally hundreds of conventions—special bidding agreements—in the bridge lexicon. These bidding agreements are put to use every day in every bridge game played anywhere in the world. Some are standard, such as Stayman and Blackwood. Some are too esoteric or exotic for words. You can learn every convention ever invented, but they won't be as useful to you as simply paying attention to the auction. Truly listening to the bidding is a skill you will need to advance in the game of bridge.

♠654   ♥AQJ654   ♦AK   ♣65

You are South.

W	N	E	S
			1♥
1♠	2♥	3♠	?

You have a fine hand, but what about those five low cards in spades and clubs? Also, partner might have raised to 2♥ with only 6 or 7 high-card points. How can you make a game with only 21 or 22 HCP between the two hands?

If you are listening to the bidding, you will know you don't have three losers in spades. You almost certainly have only one loser in that suit. Recall the bidding: Your left-hand opponent overcalled 1♠, marking him with five spades. Your right-hand opponent bid 3♠, a weak bid that guarantees at least four trumps (modern players never jump raise, either weakly or as an invitation, without at least four-card trump support). That's at least nine of the spades accounted for already. You have three. Partner can have one at the most.

There's more. Because he raised, your partner has announced at least three hearts for you. That means there is a good chance you can use a couple of them in dummy to ruff your losing spades. You have a probable six trump tricks in your hand, two potential ruffs in dummy, bringing you to eight tricks, and you also have the top two diamonds. That's ten tricks. You might go down if you bid 4♥, but the odds are greatly in your favor.

If you keep your eyes open, you'll see that many
of the secrets to happiness are right in front of you.

▷ Principle 53: Master the basics before you expand your convention repertoire.

There are four basic conventions that are more or less indispensable for any serious player: Stayman, Blackwood, transfers over 1NT and 2NT, and negative doubles. If you play none of these conventions, you will have difficulty in any game outside of party bridge.

Before you branch out into other conventional agreements, be sure you know as much as you can about the basic four. There is ample reading material available to help you brush up on these conventions, and if you are playing duplicate, there will be many experienced players around to answer your questions.

It's important to know more than just the mechanics of these basic bids. You should become familiar with the nuances as well. The negative double provides a good example. As you know, after your partner opens, if the next player makes an overcall, a double by you is not a penalty double. It is for takeout, typically describing a hand that is worth a bid but is without an appropriate one—thus the double.

♠765	♥AK54	♦J1087	♣73

W	N	E	S
	1♣	1♠	?

You have enough to respond to partner's 1♣ opener, but East's 1♠ overcall has robbed you of space and you have no appropriate bid: 2♥ shows more high-card points than you have, and it also shows at least five hearts. You can't bid 1NT because you don't have a spade stopper. You don't want to raise partner's clubs with only two of them. So the double shows a hand of modest strength without an appropriate bid.

That's easy enough, but there's a nuance with a negative double you should know.

W	N	E	S
	1♣	1♦	?

Many players use a negative double in this situation to show exactly four cards in each major. That's because the one-level major-suit bid is still available after a 1♦ overcall, so that if South bids 1♥ or 1♠ over 1♦, it would show only four and would deny holding four cards in each major.

*Whatever your discipline, a solid foundation
will serve you well as you strive to improve.*

> **Principle 54: Add conventions slowly.**

At some point in your development as a player, many of the mental tasks you must perform will become second nature to you. You won't have to make a conscious decision to do this or that—recalling the bidding, counting dummy's points, using the Rule of 11 on the opening lead, among dozens of chores—it will just happen. Until you get to that stage with quite a few of these tasks, there are so many things to think about that it's pure folly to tax your mental capacity needlessly.

One way that many players burden themselves unnecessarily is by adding too many conventions too fast.

At duplicate clubs and tournaments, players are required to fill out what is known as a "convention card." It is an accounting of the bidding agreements the partnership has made. Many of them are listed by their popular names, including those mentioned in this book so far: Stayman and Blackwood, to name two. The convention card, once it is completed by both players in the partnership, must be on display for the opponents throughout the game.

It is often a sign of an inexperienced partnership to see every space on the convention card filled out, as though they were trying to use every convention ever invented. That kind of brain overload makes for numerous errors, not to mention "forgets"—they have added so many conventions they can't remember them all. Even worse, they have added all these bidding agreements without fully understanding them. It's a chaotic situation.

Don't clutter up your mind trying to remember a handful of conventions that come up twice a year. Keep it simple, especially in the beginning, for greater enjoyment of the game and—here's a bonus—better results.

♣ ♦ ♥ ♠

Don't try to rush progress.

> **Principle 55: Know thine enemy.**

Smart players don't try to add every bidding agreement invented to their collection of bidding tools, but it's wise to strive for at least passing familiarity with a wide variety of conventions.

If you don't, you could be caught unawares.

Suppose, for example, you are in second seat and dealer on your right opens 2♦. Dealer's partner says, "Alert," which is tournament bridge lingo indicating that 2♦ doesn't mean what it sounds like. Most players use 2♦ to show a weak hand with a decent six-card suit.

The bid of 2♦, however, can have several other meanings. One of them is a convention known as Flannery, after its inventor, William Flannery. Here are the basics: A 2♦ bid shows five hearts, four spades, and 11 to 15 HCP. Responder has a variety of ways to find out more about the 2♦ opener's hand, but the 2♦ bid has no relation to diamonds. This may seem a strange use for this bid, but it has many adherents, and you are likely to run into it at a duplicate club, and especially at tournaments.

You don't have to use this convention yourself, but you must be prepared to deal with it when it comes up against you. The

Flannery defense—the method for getting into the bidding when someone opens 2♦—is not complicated or taxing on the memory, and there are different ways of approaching it. The point is to discuss it with your partner and make sure you are on the same wavelength. A simple method is to play that a double of 2♦ shows a balanced hand of about 1NT opening range (15–17), 2♠ and minor-suit bids are natural, 2NT shows both minors, leaving 2♥ as a strong takeout of hearts, something like the following hand:

♠AJ109   ♥6   ♦KQJ4   ♣AQ43

♣ ♦ ♥ ♠

When you are working with someone toward a common goal, good communication is essential.

▷ Principle 56: Avoid misuse of Blackwood.

Blackwood, the bid most players use to ask about aces in partner's hand, is at once a blessing and a curse. Many players use it to get to slam. That is the wrong approach. Blackwood, a bid of 4NT in almost everyone's system, is more appropriately used to avoid bidding slam when you are missing two aces.

The most grievous errors involving Blackwood are its use when holding two or more quick losers in a suit—or when holding a void.

♠AQJ54   ♥65   ♦KQ54   ♣A6

Your partner opens 1♠ and immediately you are thinking about slam. Many players just starting out would get so excited that they would not be able to contain themselves and would bid 4NT immediately. The problem with that is, what if partner shows one ace? You don't know what to do now. If you bid slam, partner will turn up with the following hand.

♠K10987   ♥QJ4   ♦AJ   ♣K107

There's a good chance the opponents will cash the first two heart tricks to defeat your slam. So you take the conservative route and sign off at 5♠. In that case, partner's hand will be the following:

♠K10987   ♥AK104   ♦6   ♣K107

Now slam is a near 100 percent certainty. You can't tell, of course, which hand partner has when your only contribution to the auction has been 4NT. It's much better to make whatever bid in your system represents a game-forcing spade raise so that you and partner can do some cuebidding (showing your first- and second-round controls).

The same problem occurs if you use Blackwood when you have a void in some suit other than trumps. Even if you don't have two quick losers in some third suit, you still won't know what to do if it turns out your side is missing an ace.

♣ ♦ ♥ ♠

*Know your task well enough that you can always properly
use the tools at your disposal.*

▷ Principle 57: Be careful of those doubles.

In your collection of bidding weapons, one you will use frequently is the double. Although not strictly a bid—remember, all bids are calls but not all calls are bids—the double can be used to devastating effect.

The double can keep the opponents in line. If they know you have a quick trigger finger, they will be less inclined to get involved in your auctions. Many competitive bids, after all, are right on the edge of disaster. That is the way many successful duplicate players go about their business.

The double can be a very effective lead directing bid.

♠654   ♥A6   ♦KQJ107   ♣J74

W	N	E	S
1NT	P	2♦	?

East's bid of 2♦ is a transfer, telling West to bid 2♥. This is your chance to help your partner with his decision about the opening lead, assuming East-West end up playing the contract (a good possibility, given the fact that West has announced a strong hand). If West does play the contract, you can't think of a better opening lead for partner than a diamond. If it turns out that your partner has a lot of diamonds also, you might have paved the way for a successful sacrifice against their heart contract. There are too many ways for the double of 2♦ to turn a profit for you to consider not doubling.

Bear in mind, however, that the double will allow East and West to exchange some information. The transfer bid of 2♦ shows at least five hearts, so if West does not have three of them, he can pass to so indicate. In that way, your double has given East-West an opportunity to learn something right away. Similarly, if West accepts the transfer when he didn't have to bid, he will be telling East that the partnership has at least eight hearts between them. This could be helpful if the bidding becomes competitive.

Still, double is the correct call with the South cards.

It's not likely to be good strategy to tell everything you know.

Chapter 9

Counterattacks—
When the Opponents Fire the First Shot

You know it's important to seize the initiative when you can. Your opponents are also aware that this is a good strategy, and you must be prepared to deal with them when they have gotten in the first blow. You are not without resources yourself, and you must not be timid in your approach. As long as you shun needless risks, you can counter their moves with moves of your own.

➤ Principle 58: Give up on off-shape takeout doubles.

It is understood that the opponents have an advantage when they open the bidding. They have the edge in the exchange of information so necessary to reach the best final contract.

That doesn't mean you are without resources, however. You can get into the bidding with a variety of overcalls, including those showing more than one suit at a time. There is also the takeout double, a very handy weapon if used properly. That last word is the key.

The most flagrant misuse of the takeout double involves what is known as an "off-shape" double. To many players, a double of an opening bid indicates nothing more than another opening bid, without regard to the requirement that a takeout double of one suit promises at least three-card support for the unbid suits.

♠A32   ♥KJ54   ♦KQ86   ♣65

After your right-hand opponent opens 1♠, you have no option but to pass with this hand. If you make a takeout double, partner will bid clubs a good percentage of the time. He will not be happy, holding four clubs to the jack, to see you put this hand down as dummy. If, over partner's 2♣ bid, you remove it to 2♦, you are showing a much better hand than you hold. Good players double and bid their own suits when they have very strong hands and very good suits, such as the following.

♠K6   ♥KQJ1098   ♦AQ9   ♣K10

The bottom line is that if you don't have the proper shape for a takeout double—or compensating extra strength and a long, strong suit of your own—you must go quietly. It's tough enough when the opponents get in the first lick. Don't make things worse with takeout doubles that can turn into disasters.

♣ ♦ ♥ ♠

Just because you have a weapon at your disposal,
it doesn't always mean that it is a good idea to use it.

▷ **Principle 59: Be careful when you're vulnerable.**
As much as you will want to mount a counterattack when the opponents open the bidding against you, you must beware of that condition often known as being "hot" or "red," so called because in duplicate games the trays the cards sit in have red stickers over the compass positions to indicate which side is vulnerable (the color is green if your side is not vulnerable).

As you know, if you go down in a contract when you are vulnerable, the penalty is greater—100 for each undertrick as opposed to 50. If you are doubled and go down one, the penalty is minus 200 for the first undertrick. A minus score of 200 is commonly known as the kiss of death. That's because it's very difficult to achieve a score of plus 200 playing a part score. Minus 200 is almost always a poor score.

Given the opportunity to achieve a plus 200 or better by doubling you, the opponents will do so with alacrity. In other words, they will be much more likely to double you when you step out of line in a vulnerable state than when you are not vulnerable. Further encouraging them is the fact that in a duplicate game, even if you make your doubled contract it's not the end of the world. It's just one board, with usually at least a couple of dozen others to play.

When you are vulnerable you will try to beef up those overcalls, particularly bids at the two level and higher.

♠KJ1075   ♥Q5   ♦K64   ♣J43

This is a normal overcall of 1♠ if your right-hand opponent opens 1♥. Switch the suits around, however, and you should think again.

♠K64   ♥Q5   ♦KJ1075   ♣J43

If RHO opens 1♥, you have a clear-cut pass with this hand vulnerable, and it would be stretching things even if you were not vulnerable.

♣ ♦ ♥ ♠

It's great to be brave, and even better to be brave and sensible.

➤ Principle 60: Get in there over their 1NT if you can.

When an opponent announces a strong hand, such as when 1NT is opened showing 15 to 17 HCP, the natural tendency is to be

cautious. That's a good idea in certain situations (there's that vulnerability thing again), but in the long run it's best to try to mix it
up if you have the right kind of hand.

A couple of things can happen if you are bold enough to get
into the bidding after they open 1NT. First of all, you and partner
might find a great fit in some suit. On rare occasions, you might
even make a game despite the big hand held by your opponent.
Second, it's a lot more difficult for the opponents to exchange information and make decisions when you're in there taking up bidding space. Think about the problem for the 1NT opener's partner
in the following situation:

♠A92   ♥76   ♦QJ109   ♣Q763

Your partner has opened 1NT and the next player has bid
2♥, showing hearts and a minor suit. You have 9 HCP, so the deal
belongs to your side, and you want to do something, but what? If
you double, partner will be holding a couple of low hearts himself
and you will be very lucky to defeat 2♥ despite all your high-card
points. If you bid a natural 2NT and partner has no heart stopper
(again, some poor holding in hearts), you could end up in game
and watching the opponents take the first five or six tricks. If you
pass, 2♥ could well be passed out, and you could end up unable to
defeat their contract when your side can make game (on occasions
when partner has one heart stopper and a source of tricks).

It's a whole lot easier if RHO just passes. All you have to do is
bid 2NT, natural and invitational. Much better.

Do you see now why it's important to bid over their 1NT
openers? You can get clobbered, of course, but you stand to gain a
lot more if you bid.

That doesn't mean you should be sailing in there with any old
thing. You should adopt one of the takeout systems—there are plenty
of them—discuss it with your partner and stick to the parameters.

♣ ♦ ♥ ♠

You will go nowhere without ambition.

▷ Principle 61: Stay fixed.

There will be occasions when the opposition will put you in a position from which there is no plausible escape. It is sometimes said on these occasions that you have been "fixed" in the bidding. Most of the time, it's best to stay fixed.

If you make it a practice to make bids forced on you by the opponents, you will have many more poor results than you will good ones. The fact that you are under pressure from the opponents does not change a bad bid into a good one. It's still a bad bid. In the following example, you are vulnerable against nonvulnerable opponents. Your left-hand opponent opens 1♣, your partner passes, and the next player bids 3♠, showing a long suit and a weak hand. You are looking at the following cards:

♠J   ♥AK764   ♦Q32   ♣K743

The 3♠ bid is an unusual treatment, one unlikely to be found at other tables, and you are tempted to bid 4♥ to combat this annoying development. You are, to be sure, fixed. If you pass, your partner might turn up with a pretty good hand—or a bad hand.

With a chunkier suit (or perhaps extra length), it would make more sense to bid, but it could still work out very badly. The best policy in situations of this kind is to pass. Just stay fixed. Partner will be happier if he's not forced to watch you going down, doubled, every time an opponent makes an aggressive bid.

There are other, more common situations, such as sitting in second seat when opener starts the bidding at the three level or higher. It's normal to be tempted to bid "just to show them." That's falling into their trap. No matter how you dress it up, a bad bid is a bad bid.

You have to accept that it's not possible to
make lemonade every time life deals you a lemon.

> **Principle 62: Don't make bids based on likely misdefense.**

You will, from time to time, find yourself playing against opponents you consider your inferiors. They might well be, but you should be slow to judge your opponents as to their competence. Not everyone you meet will be as confident as you are.

One of the worst breaches of discipline you can perpetrate is to make a bid predicated on the likelihood that your opponents will screw up the defense or that you can trick them. Even if you get away with one of these every now and then, your partner will be watching and noting your bad bids.

You can tell a lot about a person by how he acts when he thinks no one is looking.

> **Principle 63: Remember that points don't take tricks.**

In the competitive world of bridge, you will be faced with a lot of interference by the opposition. Just as you want to foul up their auctions and rob them of bidding space, they have the same goals where you are concerned. There will even be times when you will have the great preponderance of the high-card points and still find the opponents flitting around in your auctions like gnats. Be careful when you go to swat at them—by doubling, mostly—that you have the right ammunition to do the job.

The reference here is to the lame practice of doubling the opponents based on your high-card points rather than trump tricks.

This following deal occurred in a bridge game in Houston, Texas:

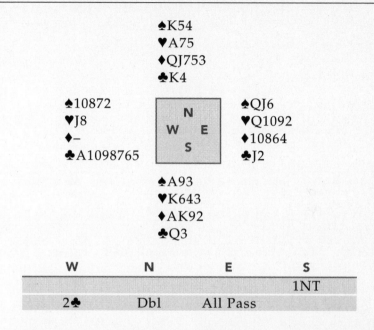

♠K54
♥A75
♦QJ753
♣K4

♠10872   ♠QJ6
♥J8   ♥Q1092
♦−   ♦10864
♣A1098765   ♣J2

♠A93
♥K643
♦AK92
♣Q3

W	N	E	S
			1NT
2♣	Dbl	All Pass	

This was the classic case of doubling on points—unsuccess-fully. North knew his side had a minimum 28 HCP (1NT showed 15–17). In fact, North-South had a total of 29 HCP—and no chance of defeating 2♣. North started with a diamond and West ruffed. He then banged down the ♣A and played another club, watching with amusement when the ♣K and ♣Q butted heads. From there, North-South could take two tricks in each of the majors, but nothing else. That was minus 180 for North-South when they could easily have made ten tricks in 3NT. North fell into the trap of doubling a trump contract without trump tricks. Even if 2♣ had somehow been defeated by one trick, it would not have compensated for the bonus North-South were due for simply bidding their no-trump game.

Although players double unsuccessfully on high-card points all the time and again and again, some never learn the lesson. You will be way ahead of the game if you remember that trump tricks—not HCP—are needed to defeat trump contracts.

Don't take a penknife to a sword fight.

▷ Principle 64: Double to "protect" your part score.

When you are playing in a duplicate game or a tournament, there will be times when you will face a close decision as to whether you should double your opponents, bid on, or just pass. When you have been outbid in a competitive auction, a factor in determining whether you should bid on will be whether you can make it if you "take the push," so to speak. That's not all you have to consider, however.

The fate of your "other" contract—the one you were in before you were outbid—will also be a consideration. If you judge that you were going to make the lower-level contract, but you don't think you can make a contract one level higher, it will often pay off for you to double the opponents. In that sense, you are attempting to make up for the contract you believe you would have made before the opponents went one level higher.

♠965	♥A632	◆A7	♣9754

W	N	E	S
	1♠	2◆	2♠
3◆	P	P	?

You are South with the hand above in this auction. Both sides are vulnerable. Your partner has opened the bidding and heard you raise to 2♠, and has opted not to compete further in the face of the opponents' bidding. What is your decision?

First, you must ask yourself whether you have a shot at 3♠. The law of total tricks tells you not to bid on. The general rule is that you should not contract for a number of tricks that exceeds the number of trumps between the two hands. If your partner had six spades, it is likely he would have competed to 3♠. He knows, after all, that you have at least three spades for your raise. He is leaving it up to you, in case you have four spades, to decide whether your side should bid on.

You have only three spades—not very good ones, either—plus dull shape. It is very unlikely, if partner cannot bid again, that you can take nine tricks in spades. You do have two cards that are good for defense, however—your two aces. Even so, with everybody bidding, there is no guarantee you will defeat 3♦, but if you pass and you do defeat it one trick, you will receive a poor score. It is likely that you would have made your 2♠ contract, which would have produced a score of plus 110. If you defeat 3♦ one trick, that's only 100, which will be a poor score, possibly even a zero. You must double to "protect" your plus 110. If you defeat 3♦, your score will be plus 200, more than adequate compensation.

You hope the layout of the cards is something like the following:

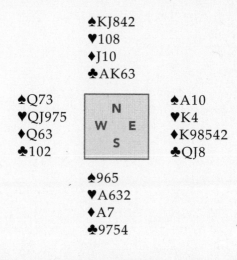

                    ♠KJ842
                    ♥108
                    ♦J10
                    ♣AK63
    ♠Q73   ♠A10
    ♥QJ975   N   ♥K4
    ♦Q63   W   E   ♦K98542
    ♣102   S   ♣QJ8
                    ♠965
                    ♥A632
                    ♦A7
                    ♣9754

As you can see, your partner's limit in a spade contract is eight tricks, but you can defeat 3♦ by one trick. You lead a spade, establishing a trick in that suit—and you still have two high clubs plus two red aces to come. That's five tricks and plus 200—so long as you doubled. If you look closely at the East-West hands, you will note that not everyone will bid with the East cards. The long suit, after all, is not exactly robust. That means many North-South pairs will be left to play 2♠, and they will score plus 110 pretty easily. If your plus on this deal is only 100, you will have a lousy score.

When it comes to protecting what is yours, you do
what is necessary even if it might be unpleasant.

Chapter 10

Situational Strategy—
When the "Wrong" Move Can Be Right

Bridge has lots of principles that seem like absolutes: lead fourth best, count your tricks, always have your bids. The list goes on and on. Just when you think you're getting a handle on all that, someone tells you it's right to do the opposite sometimes. It's tough to sort out when to go against the grain. Don't try to rush it, and don't be discouraged if it takes some time.

➤ Principle 65: Understand "swinging."

There will be times when you feel you need to manufacture a good result. It may come during a string of bad results—you simply want to stop the bleeding. You might judge, late in a session, that you are close to a first-place finish, but you need to finish with a bang. You may simply have a feeling about a particular deal. Something tells you to go for it.

Understand that there are boundaries here. It is unfair to the other players in the game if you make insane bids and plays in an attempt to create top scores. More likely, you would be handing out "gifts" all over the room, and you can be disciplined for overdoing it.

Swinging is much more subtle than just blasting away. Keep in mind, also, that you are not the only person involved. You have a partner sitting across the table from you.

If you are playing with someone who believes that coming in second or third is very respectable, he will not appreciate a series of wild moves that drops you out of the money altogether, especially if he had no say in the matter. Above all else, bridge is a partnership game. If your approach to competition is that only first place is worthy, bridge might be the wrong arena for you.

♣ ♦ ♥ ♠

The pursuit itself is often an ample reward.
You don't always have to come in first to feel successful.

▷ Principle 66: Know how to swing.

You are in the final round of a pair game and it seems you and your partner have had a decent, if not spectacular, game. You feel that if you could get a top score on one of the last two deals, you would have an excellent chance to come in first. You are prepared to risk dropping in the standings for a shot at the top spot. Your partner is along for the ride, within reason.

First of all, you will need some luck. If the last two deals are more or less routine, you might not be able to do better than just a bit above average. If fortune smiles on you, one of the last two deals will give you something to work with.

♠AJ108   ♥AK954   ♦J64   ♣4

You are South and your side is vulnerable.

W	N	E	S
			1♥
1♠	2♥	2♠	?

Your prospects for game are not particularly good if the best your partner could do was raise to 2♥. Your spade cards are decidedly ill-placed, being "in front" of the player who overcalled 1♠. You know something they don't, however—that spades are breaking very badly. Ordinarily, you would look on the vulnerability—you are, they are not—as an advantage for them. You can be pretty sure that a heart game for your side would be a struggle at best, but the opponents don't know that. If you are up for a slight risk, leap to 4♥ directly over East's 2♠ bid.

To West, it sounds like you're an odds-on favorite, and he is likely to take out some insurance, so to speak. He'll take the favorable vulnerability save of 4♠, expecting it to be profitable even if he goes down three tricks doubled for minus 500. After all, you sound like you are cold for game in hearts, which would score 620.

You will, of course, double 4♠ and collect plus 300 to 500 barring really foul breaks. Your score will look very good against what the other players are managing, probably plus 110 or 140, maybe even plus 170 for taking ten tricks but not bidding game.

In ordinary circumstances, you would not take this chance. If West passed you in 4♥, after all, you might be left to flounder there, going down two or three tricks.

There is an important consideration. If you know West to be a very conservative player, don't try this gambit. If he is a normal, competitive duplicate player, it's a reasonable shot.

♣ ♦ ♥ ♠

Experience will teach you when bold moves have the best chance of paying off.

➤ Principle 67: Size up the field.

There are some important factors to keep in mind as you attempt to estimate how your session is going. One key factor is the strength of the field. If you are playing in a club game in which most of the players are relatively new, you can count on pretty good results any time your private scorecard has lots of pluses. There should be no need for fancy moves in that case.

At the same time, if the field is somewhat weak and an opponent works out a difficult line of play to land a close game, you can count on a poor score. In a weak field, if you bid a slam and go down, you will get next to nothing for your aggressiveness. In fact, if your general style is aggressive and the cards do not favor pushy bidding for that session, don't bother trying to make anything up at the end of the game. There's no hope.

If you perceive that there are a number of good pairs in the game, you will be more apt to try for that little extra late in the game if you are close to winning.

You won't be able to assess the strength of every game you play in, but when it's possible the knowledge will help you formulate your strategy.

♣　♦　♥　♠

To wage the most effective campaign, you must know your opponents.

➤ Principle 68: Take advantage of the "anti-field" factor.

One way to swing, as it were, on virtually every board is to play what is known as an "anti-field" bidding system.

Chief among these is the Precision system, in which the 1♣ opener is always artificial, saying nothing about clubs, but indicating a hand with at least 16 high-card points.

When you play Precision or another so-called big club system, 1♦ becomes a kind of catch-all bid. The system also features five-card majors, normal 1NT openers, and 2♣ as a natural, limited bid, usually with at least six in the suit. That means that you frequently open the bidding with 1♦ on hands of the following types.

♠AQ65   ♥QJ4   ♦52   ♣A1098
♠AQ10   ♥KQJ   ♦72   ♣J7643
♠AJ43   ♥A1097   ♦43   ♣KQJ

Some Precision pairs even agree to open 1♦ with a singleton in the suit.

Without going into the merits of opening 1♦ on singletons and weak doubletons, such a bid often has the effect of "picking off" a legitimate diamond suit possessed by an opponent.

Some Precision pairs employ a 1NT opener of 13–15 HCP, which can have the effect, as demonstrated in Chapter 4, of making declarer the exact opposite of most pairs. The 2♣ opener is also sufficiently unusual that, combined with the other features of Precision, the auction at your table will be decidedly different from others.

There are other "different" kinds of bidding systems, including Acol, a chiefly British system employing four-card majors and so-called Acol two-bids: long-strong suits.

Kaplan-Sheinwold is another system featuring "weak" 1NT openers, and then there is the legendary EHAA system—Every Hand An Adventure. Weak two-bids can be made on five-card suits, with a range of 6–12 HCP, and the 1NT opener is 10–12. It's strictly for players with strong stomachs and a tolerance for big numbers.

The choices are plentiful if marching to the beat of a different drummer is your idea of fun. Be forewarned that anti-field systems can make for some very big games—but also some very bad ones.

In the end, of course, the game is still about tricks and taking the most that you can, regardless of the system you play.

♣ ♦ ♥ ♠

Being out of step with the world is not necessarily bad. If you can handle the negatives, the positives will be rewarding.

▷ Principle 69: Embrace anti-field plays.

Another way to go for the extra matchpoints (for those who don't know, those are the points you strive for in duplicate games) is to make anti-field plays. You can't really build such a thing into a system, and you have to keep an eye out for the opportunities.

An example of a play calculated to score a lot or a little would involve a nine-card holding in a suit missing the queen, ♠AJ1054 opposite ♠K983, for example.

You know that most declarers, particularly in a field with lots of inexperienced players, will play for the drop, adhering to the "eight ever, nine never" rule about finessing. Since getting an extra trick can make a major difference in your matchpoint score, you might consider finessing, and try to figure out which of your opponents might hold the queen. If you finesse and it's right, you can count on a very good score.

What you must try to judge is whether the contract you are in will be pretty much standard around the room. If it's a normal contract and you got a normal lead, then judge whether it's worth the chance. Considering the eight-ever-nine-never rule, you might also reject the standard finesse for the queen when you hold only eight of the suit.

Sometimes you will reject a normal play because you don't want it to work, such as when you perceive that your bidding has gone awry and you have missed a better contract that most players will find. For example, if you think everyone will be in slam with ♠AJ1054 opposite ♠K983, and you have failed to bid the slam, you might finesse even with nine, hoping that it's the correct play on this particular deal. If so, slam will go down at most of the tables where it is bid. You have lost out in the bidding, and it won't matter if those pairs play for the drop and it works. You will still lose. If a finesse is necessary, however, you will beat all the players in slam who don't guess right as well as the ones in game who make the normal play.

♣ ♦ ♥ ♠

It's exciting to take chances, but prudent to know when the time is right.

➤ Principle 70: Don't swing against inexperienced players.

When you are up against players who are clearly inexperienced, it will pay to play it down the middle most of the time. Don't be superaggressive or "cute" in the bidding with the idea of bamboozling your opponents. In many cases, they will do the wrong thing if only you let them. Wild preemptive bidding or bullying will cause them to clam up. You could easily be left holding the bag with your silly jump bids or psychics. Remember, too, that if you let the opponents play the contract, they are likely to take fewer tricks than others, which will be a source of matchpoints for you without any risk.

♣ ♦ ♥ ♠

A feeling of superiority is not a guarantee of success, especially if it causes you to stray from the correct path.

➤ Principle 71: Be aware of the form of scoring.

The decisions you make will be affected to a large extent by the form of scoring. In most matchpoint contests, your objective is to outscore all the other pairs who hold the same cards as you. Your true opponents are the pairs sitting the same direction you are sitting—East-West or North-South. The players you face at the table are there to help or hinder you in your quest to do better than the pairs sitting your direction.

In pair games, you might well risk your contract for an overtrick. If your quest for an overtrick succeeds, you will do very well because most players will not take the risk. Of course, if you don't make the overtrick and go down trying, you will do very poorly for the same reason.

At pairs, you will double the opponents much more readily. In most pair games, you will play approximately twenty-five deals. If you double and they make it, you will get a zero, but it's only one-twenty-fifth of your overall score. If you compensate with top scores, it won't hurt to have a couple of zeros.

If you are playing in a team game, however, the situation is much different. Matches are usually only seven deals or so, and the comparisons are made only between two tables. A major disaster can mean a loss.

In a rubber bridge game, your contract is sacred. You will sacrifice any and all overtricks just to be sure you make what you bid. Party bridge, though far less serious in the implications for losing, is much the same.

It's tough to work out your objective if you don't know the basic ground rules. Take the time to understand your task.

Chapter 11

Taking Risks

No one in any sport succeeds by playing down the middle all the time. That's why football coaches decide to go for it on fourth down or try fake punts. That's why baseball players try to steal bases or swing for home runs. The winners are usually the competitors who are willing to let it all hang out on occasion. On the other hand, you don't see football teams throwing Hail Mary passes on every down, so some measure of conservatism is in order. The same is true in bridge. If you are not willing to risk looking foolish, your results will be steady but lackluster. The key, as with most competitive exercises, is picking your spots.

> **Principle 72: Don't take rash actions.**

Sometimes you must stray from the norm or take the aggressive tactics up a notch. That's part of the strategy of trying to improve your scores, particularly late in the game when you think it will give you a chance to win.

Swinging, in this sense, does not mean taking leave of your senses.

First of all, it's not likely to work. Even the most inexperienced of your opponents knows enough to double when you are completely out of line. Even if they don't double and you are really out of line, you'll get a terrible score all by yourself. Second, if your partner sees you over there losing your mind, he'll wonder why he agreed to play with you. If you get a reputation as a madman, you'll have trouble getting partners. Third, it's against the spirit of the game to go around "throwing boards," as duplicate players put it.

♣ ♦ ♥ ♠

Don't let emotion control you. Think before you act.

➤ Principle 73: Don't try to "make up" for a disaster.

There will be times when things go wrong for you at the table. In many, if not most, of them, it will be crystal clear that a "disaster" has occurred. Perhaps it will be a moment of inattention on your part—maybe even partner's—that allows an opponent's hopeless game to be made. It might be that you have just gone down 1100 in a save against a nonmaking game. Now and then, you will bid a ridiculous game or slam and go down what feels like a million tricks.

The worst thing you can do after getting a bad board is to try to make up for it on the very next deal. In 99 out of 100 cases, you will find yourself with two disasters to overcome—and it can snowball into a nightmare of a game. This kind of thing saps your confidence, hurts your partnership, and is simply a miserable way to conduct the business of playing bridge.

You can't just "swing" for a good result whenever you want. It's a matter of recognizing the opportunity and seizing it—if you have the stomach for the potential bad result that can go along with the attempt. Face it, everything you do isn't going to work out— and you can't manufacture opportunities for big scores whenever you want.

Keep your wits about when you when suffer a reverse.

> **Principle 74: Don't play partner for the perfect hand.**

The late Barry Crane, arguably the greatest matchpoint player of all time, was legendary for his "rules." He believed, for example, that if you were trying to guess the location of a queen and you had a two-way guess—say, KJ3 in dummy and A105 in your hand—the rank of the suit involved made a difference. If it was a minor-suit queen, Crane believed it was correct to play for the queen to be "over" the jack, or to the right of the KJ3. The correct play was to cash the king and play low to the 10. If the queen was in a major suit, declarer should play for the queen to be "in front" of the jack, or to the left of the KJ3: play the ace, then low to the jack.

That rule of Crane's might seem silly to some, but most everyone subscribes to another of his most famous pronouncements to his partners: "Never play me for the perfect hand. I won't have it."

♠AK5   ♥KQJ10987   ♦4   ♣A2

You are South.

W	N	E	S
	1♦	P	1♥
P	2♥	P	4NT
P	5♥	P	5NT
P	6♦	P	?

Your 4NT bid asked partner about his aces, and 5♥ said he had two. Your 5NT bid asked about kings, and partner admitted to holding one. If he had two, you would be able to count thirteen tricks and you would simply bid 7NT. It's so great to be able to bid a grand slam, but can you do it here?

Well, partner might have the right hand, perhaps one of the following two:

♠Q43   ♥A543   ♦AJ108   ♣K6
♠62   ♥A543   ♦AJ108   ♣KQ5

In the first case, the ♠Q would be your thirteenth trick, in the second, the ♣Q would do the honors.

Either one, or many variations thereto, would be the perfect hand. There are many other hands partner could hold for the bidding, and since you can't find out about these random queens, you would be foolhardy to contract for all thirteen tricks. Remember, especially if you are playing duplicate, that none of the others holding your two hands will be able to find out what they need to know to be sure of a grand slam—and hardly anyone will bid it. If you do, and you go down, you will suffer the fate you deserve.

On many occasions, you will find that your wisest course is to go for the best result possible rather than the best possible result.

▷ Principle 75: Don't be afraid of looking foolish.

Just when you think you have the game of bridge figured out—usually after a really good session—it has a way of bringing you crashing back to earth. Those wonderful, flawless guesses you were making today might all be wrong tomorrow.

That's part of the allure of the game. No matter how long you play or how good you get, you will never master it. But it sure is fun to try.

You will do many things inadvertently to make yourself look foolish. Why, you ask, would you do something on purpose that could make you look the same way?

It's because you must sometimes be bold to feel the exhilaration of the supreme moment that ends with everyone at the table saying, "Wow! You played the heck out of that contract."

The following deal was played by Nashville expert Chuck Said many years ago. He risked looking foolish but ended up with a magnificent effort that is beautiful to behold.

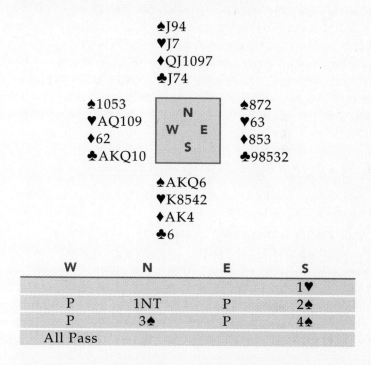

	W	N	E	S
				1♥
	P	1NT	P	2♠
	P	3♠	P	4♠
All Pass				

West started with the ♣K, continuing with the ♣A. Said considered his play for some time before he proceeded—in a way you might not conceive even looking at all four hands.

Said ruffed with the ♠Q, played his low diamond to dummy's queen, and ruffed the third club with the ♠K. Now he cashed the ♠A and the ♦A; then he played a spade to dummy's 9, breathing a huge sigh of relief when it held. Finally, he cashed the ♠J and pitched the ♦K from his hand. With that card out of the way, he was able to run dummy's last three diamonds. He took two club ruffs in hand, one high trump in hand, two trumps in dummy (the 9 and jack), and a total of five diamond tricks. That was ten tricks and a great score.

You can see, of course, that as the cards lie, Said could have ruffed low and simply led a low heart from hand toward dummy's jack. But that requires West to have both heart honors. It was much simpler for Said to play for West to have the ♠10.

Said risked a pair of red cheeks if his play of a spade to the 9 had lost to the 10, but he knows that no matter what you do or how well you play, at some point bridge will make you look foolish anyway. It's those moments when the ♠9 holds that make the risk worthwhile.

In assessing the risks of a big gamble, it's important to know whether the feeling you'll have if it pays off makes up for the possible pain of failure.

▷ Principle 76: Learn to play smoothly.

If you're going to take a few chances for those great payoffs, it will be in your best interest to cultivate a smooth manner. Your gambles in the bidding and the play will be much more effective if your opponents don't know you are way out there on the end of the limb.

The way to keep the opposition from picking up on your secret is to plan your moves ahead of time and make them in what seems to be a perfectly natural rhythm. You will spoil it if you are obviously in dire straits or clearly taking a big shot.

♠AKQJ6   ♥AQ8765   ♦43   ♣–

You are South.

W	N	E	S
			1♥
P	2♥	2NT	?

East's 2NT bid shows nine or ten cards in the minors.

You have such a powerful hand once partner shows support for your heart suit that a contract of 6♥ might well be unbeatable. The problem is that it's going to be very difficult to determine whether there is a diamond control without pinpointing the lead for the opponents. If you cuebid everything under the sun except for diamonds, you can be sure that's the lead you will get.

You could give up on slam and just bid 4♥—or you could just blast your way to 6♥ and hope, in the event they have a couple of quick tricks in diamonds, that they don't find the lead. If you stew about it and finally jump to 6♥, you will be alerting the opponents that you have a problem. They will stand a better chance of working out the right thing to do.

If you bid the slam seemingly without a care in the world, you have a better chance of success.

Even better would be to throw some figurative sand in their eyes, perhaps leaping to 4♦ yourself to indicate a control in that suit. They might believe you and lead something else. There's a good chance they will believe you if you make your move without hemming and hawing about it.

♣ ♦ ♥ ♠

Always project confidence, even when you don't feel it.

➤ Principle 77: Don't swing at experts.
One of the great aspects of tournament bridge is that you have the opportunity to play against some of the best players in the world. There are probably fifty or so players who are regulars at tournaments who can also count themselves as current or past world champions. The United States has a very good record in international competition, so it's very possible that you would come up against one or more of these superstars.

As an aside, most large tournaments are set up in such a way that less-experienced players do not mix with the superstars, but there will be some events you can enter if you enjoy playing against the best.

When you sit down at the table against someone with an international reputation, you can expect him or her to play well. That doesn't mean you have no chance, however. It is possible for you to get the better of an expert pair—so long as you keep your wits about you.

The worst thing you can do is to "take a swing" at an expert. The harder you try to get the better of them through trickery—underleading an ace against a suit contract, for example—or wild bidding, the worse you will do. They have seen all the shenanigans a thousand times before. Nothing you do will surprise them—and they will make you pay for your rash actions.

Some players feel that it's worth it if one out of a hundred of their maneuvers works out against a top player. They dine out on that moment forever. They are losers. Sooner or later, a player like that will be taking swings at you because, with a steady and sensible game plan, you will eclipse him and establish yourself as superior.

Rather than throwing haymakers at the experts, study their moves and emulate them. You may not get the best of the top players often, but if the right set of hands comes along and you take advantage, you can have one of those magical moments to talk about for a long time.

♣ ♦ ♥ ♠

Everyone wants to take down the champ.
Smart people want to learn how he got to the top.

▶ Principle 78: Don't be afraid of close doubles.

When you are playing rubber or party bridge at home or in a team game in duplicate, you must be very careful about doubling part scores. Any part score above 2♦ will convert to game if made, and "doubling them into game" is a cardinal sin.

At pairs, however, it is said with validity that if you never double the opponents into game, you aren't doubling enough.

You will find when you are playing for matchpoints that the opponents will be bidding a lot more and taking more chances themselves. If you are always taking the push, bidding one more when the opponents balance or compete, you will only embolden them.

If you stop and double once in a while, especially when you know they are out of line, the opposition will be less likely to mess around in your auctions. Everyone is willing to take chances, but if they know you will pound them when they go too far, they will pull back.

Don't be afraid to take a reasonable chance. Few things in life are guaranteed.

Chapter 12

Tricks—The Essence of the Game

It should never be far from your consciousness that bridge is about tricks. You conduct auctions with the goal of finding the contract likely to produce the most tricks for your side. When you are a defender, your goal in most cases is to take enough tricks to defeat the contract. You will learn lots about high-card points, distribution, and conventions, but in the final analysis you must take tricks to succeed.

> **Principle 79: Be sure you know the basics of card play.**

A basketball player going to the free throw line does not want to have to think about what he's doing. The more the act of shooting a free throw is second nature to him, the better his chances of hitting a high percentage of those shots. That's why you see many players spending hours and hours at the free throw line. If it's more or less an automatic action, it will work better.

Good bridge players approach much of declarer play in the same fashion. They know proper technique so well that they don't have to think about it. They can save their mental energy for the times when deep thought or deduction is required to bring home a very difficult contract. That's one of the key differences between the expert and the aspiring player.

You are already familiar with lots of concepts relating to declarer play—leading up to high cards, unblocking suits, ruffing losers before pulling trumps. There are many other plays that are simple and part of an expert's repertoire that, with practice and study, you will make part of yours.

Here is an example:

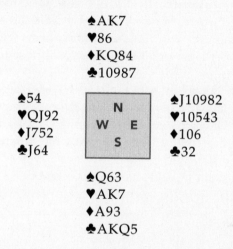

♠AK7
♥86
♦KQ84
♣10987

♠54
♥QJ92
♦J752
♣J64

♠J10982
♥10543
♦106
♣32

♠Q63
♥AK7
♦A93
♣AKQ5

You find yourself in the ambitious contract of 7NT. West leads the ♥Q and you win the ace. If clubs and diamonds behave, you have thirteen top tricks. You start with the top two clubs, and when both opponents follow you know that suit will produce four tricks for you. If diamonds are lying 3-3, you have thirteen tricks, but the odds favor a 4-2 break. There are still chances, however.

You cash the top three spades. West discards a heart on the third spade, so you know that East started with five. Now you play the ♣Q and a club to the 10, West pitching a second heart. You return to hand with the ♥K, West following with the jack, and it's looking very much as though West started with two spades, four hearts, three clubs, and therefore four diamonds.

That leaves East with five spades, four hearts, two clubs, and two diamonds.

You play a diamond to the king and another to your ace, noting that East played the 10. You now have the spots to pick up the diamond suit and take the rest of the tricks—if the first diamond you played to dummy was the 9. An expert would make this play routinely. If you did not, you are in the soup. You can play the 9 from hand and let it ride, but you will still be in your hand and will have concede a heart trick to East. If you overtake with dummy's ♦Q, the ♦8 will lose to West's jack at the end.

If you had played the ♦9 to start with, you would be left with the 3, which you could play to the 8 in the end. The ♦Q would be trick thirteen. Playing the 9 rather than the 3 seems like a small thing, but it looms pretty large when it's the difference between making a grand slam and going down.

Make it a habit to study card play technique so that you will recognize similar situations when they arise. Review your material on a regular basis to keep it second nature to you.

♣ ♦ ♥ ♠

If you want to be able to do something well, invest the time to do it naturally.

▷ Principle 80: Be flexible in your game plan.

As you hone your skills in dummy play, you will become better and better at reading the cards—determining who has what so that you can figure out the best way to achieve your objective.

Most of the time, of course, your target will be to make your contract. Even in a pairs game, where the overtricks can be very important, more often than not you will aim first and foremost at achieving a plus score.

You will, of course, acquire the habit of making a game plan before you play the first card from dummy. That's the mark of a good player: Your objective is clear and you have a plan for achieving it. You never play randomly.

There will be many times when it is necessary for you to change your game plan because of what you learn as play progresses.

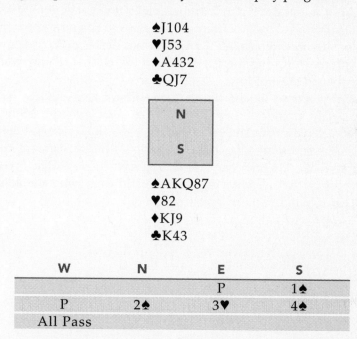

♠J104
♥J53
♦A432
♣QJ7

N
S

♠AKQ87
♥82
♦KJ9
♣K43

W	N	E	S
		P	1♠
P	2♠	3♥	4♠
All Pass			

With the South hand, after partner raises you to 2♠, you would like to make a delicate game try to see if he is at the top of his bid. When East butts in with 3♥, you don't have the opportunity. You could double 3♥, but that's dangerous policy with two low trumps. Also, you must have a shot at game with your fine hand.

West leads the ♥4. East wins the ♥A and returns the suit to West's king. A third heart goes to dummy's jack and East's queen, and you ruff. Trumps are pulled in three rounds, East showing up with two.

It looks as though the contract will depend on the diamond finesse, but there's no hurry there. After pulling the last trump, you lead a low club to dummy's queen and East's ace. A heart knocks out your last trump. Now what?

Your initial game plan included playing a diamond to the ace and a diamond to the jack, the percentage play. You now know that cannot succeed. Remember, East passed as dealer and has shown up with the ♥AQ and the ♣A. If he had the ♦Q as well, he would have opened the bidding.

Fortunately, you have the ♦9 to go with the king and jack. Your correct play in your revised game plan is to table the ♦J, letting it ride if West plays low. You know this will work. If West covers the ♦J with the queen, you will win the ace and play a low diamond from dummy to the 9 in your hand. *Voilà!* You have made a difficult contract because you were paying attention and were willing to adjust your game plan. See the complete deal below.

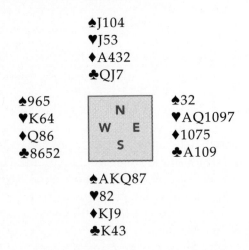

```
                    ♠J104
                    ♥J53
                    ♦A432
                    ♣QJ7
  ♠965              N              ♠32
  ♥K64           W     E          ♥AQ1097
  ♦Q86              S              ♦1075
  ♣8652                            ♣A109
                    ♠AKQ87
                    ♥82
                    ♦KJ9
                    ♣K43
```

A further note about the auction: East's 3♥ bid is typical of what you will encounter in a duplicate game. Considered in isolation,

East's bid is very dangerous, but many players would make it as a way of pushing North-South a level higher or indicating an opening lead.

♣ ♦ ♥ ♠

A plan of action that works in one set of circumstances may be a flop in another.
You hurt only yourself when you stubbornly cling to an ineffective approach.

➤ Principle 81: Train yourself to follow all the spots.

There is nothing more frustrating and confidence-sapping than arriving at some juncture in the play and being unable to remember what partner or declarer played two tricks before. It's annoying to realize you might not even have been looking. The missing information can be as significant as whether declarer followed suit at some point—or a spot card partner played that might have indicated whether he liked or disliked some suit.

Believe it or not, this happens to experienced players as well as to beginners. It's not easy to keep your head in the game trick after trick after trick. Even so, you must continue to try. As you progress and get better and better at this aspect of bridge play, your confidence will increase and the practice of watching the spots will become second nature to you.

The best way to cultivate this habit is to start with trick one. When West leads the ♠6, "say" the card in your mind, and repeat with the spot you play from dummy, then again with the card that East plays, and finally to your own card. It may seem at first as though you will never master this part, but don't be discouraged. The more you practice it, the easier it will get.

♣ ♦ ♥ ♠

The smallest details at the beginning of a project
are often the ones that loom largest at its completion.

> **Principle 82: Don't be too anxious to take a finesse.**

When you start off in bridge, discovering the finesse is exciting. As you progress in your development, it will be just as thrilling when you discover how to make your contract without relying on a finesse.

There will be many opportunities for avoiding finesses, but you must keep your eyes open for them.

♠KQJ8
♥54
♦A62
♣AK104

```
┌───────────┐
│     N     │
│           │
│     S     │
└───────────┘
```

♠A1097
♥AJ
♦KJ4
♣QJ73

You find yourself in a contract of 6♠. West leads the ♥K. You win the ace and pull trumps in three rounds. Looks like you need a successful diamond finesse to take twelve tricks, right? Not if you have studied your card play technique. Simply play off all your clubs and exit with the ♥J. West is marked with the ♥Q, so he will be left on play after winning it. What can he do? If he plays a diamond, you will let it run around to your hand. If he plays a heart, you will ruff in dummy and discard a diamond from your hand. Either way, you have your twelve tricks—and without finessing. You don't even care who has the ♦Q.

Many situations will not be as simple and easy to spot, but you will never detect them if you look first to a finesse to make your contract. Make the finesse your last choice if at all possible.

♣ ♦ ♥ ♠

Look twice at any approach that seems too easy.

➤ Principle 83: Use your imagination.

If you play long enough, you will find yourself in many a hopeless contract. As you get better and better, you will look back on some of those contracts you thought had no chance—and realize that you could have done better if only you had used your imagination.

Say you find yourself in 6♠ on the following two hands:

♠543
♥Q76
♦K543
♣AK4

```
┌──────────┐
│    N     │
│          │
│    S     │
└──────────┘
```

♠KQJ10087
♥A
♦A1086
♣Q3

You have an inevitable loser in trumps and you have no losers in hearts or clubs, but the diamond situation is a problem. You seem to have a loser there with no chance of getting rid of it. You can pitch one losing diamond from your hand on a high club, but you are still left with a loser in the suit. Looks like there's no hope, right?

Wrong.

There are four chances to make this contract if you just use your imagination. The first is that someone might have a doubleton ♥K. You simply play the ace and ruff a heart. If the king is doubleton, it will fall and the ♥Q will be trick number twelve. Second is that one of your opponents holds the ♦QJ doubleton. Third is that West has a singleton ♦Q or ♦J. You can play over to the king and finesse the 10 on the way back. The fourth possibility is that the same player holds the ♥K and three or four diamonds. In that case, he will be squeezed when you run your winners, as would be the case if the following were the full deal:

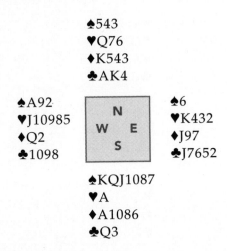

```
                    ♠543
                    ♥Q76
                    ♦K543
                    ♣AK4
   ♠A92                            ♠6
   ♥J10985          N              ♥K432
   ♦Q2            W   E            ♦J97
   ♣1098            S              ♣J7652
                    ♠KQJ1087
                    ♥A
                    ♦A1086
                    ♣Q3
```

West leads the ♥J to the 5, 4, and ace. You play the ♠K to West's ace, and he continues with the ♥10, which you ruff. The first and least likely of the chances, a doubleton ♥K, has not materialized, so you must play for other chances. If West has a singleton diamond honor or if either opponent has a doubleton ♦QJ, that condition will still exist after you try for the squeeze, so you rattle off three club tricks and four more spade tricks, coming down to the singleton ♥Q and doubleton ♦K5 in dummy, with the ♦A108 in your hand. West holds both his diamonds and a heart. East, however, is in the meat grinder. He must make a discard from ♥K and ♦J97. He is toast. If he throws the ♥K, your queen in dummy is the twelfth trick. So he must discard a diamond. Now both opponents have two diamonds, and when you play the king and then another diamond, the trick will be ♦5, ♦J, ♦A, ♦Q. Your ♦10 is now good.

A contract that looked like it had no chance has come home because you imagined different ways that it might take and played for one or more of those chances.

♣ ♦ ♥ ♠

*It's amazing what a fertile imagination can
produce in the realm of problem solving.*

> **Principle 84: Never give up.**

There's a famous saying in sports that "it ain't over 'til it's over." That is true in bridge as well. Learn to play with dogged determination. Never give up, even when things seem the most hopeless. This can apply to individual deals or to competition against seemingly superior pairs and teams. Here is a deal played by Bob Hamman, the world's No. 1 player when he was an up-and-comer forty years ago, going against one of the top players in the country, Lew Mathe (later to become Hamman's partner).

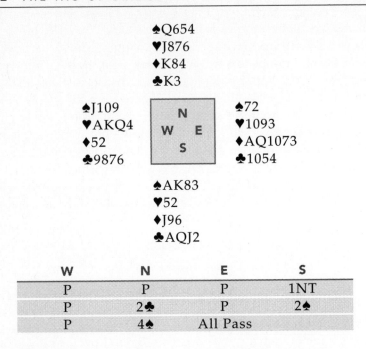

W	N	E	S
P	P	P	1NT
P	2♣	P	2♠
P	4♠	All Pass	

Mathe was West, Hamman South. His 1NT opener showed 15–17 high-card points. Mathe started with two top hearts as East signaled that he held three of them. Hamman correctly perceived from the way he played the hearts that Mathe had started with the AKQ. Since West had passed originally, he could not have the ♦A (that would have given him 13 high-card points, enough to open the bidding). Therefore, it would be suicide for Hamman to try leading up to dummy's ♦K.

Did that mean the contract was hopeless? By no means. Hamman was and still is the kind of player who never gives up. At trick three, Mathe switched to the ♠J, giving Hamman a chance (obviously, a diamond switch would have defeated the contract). Hamman won in dummy, ruffed a heart in his hand, cashed the ♠A and ran four clubs, pitching two diamonds from dummy. This was the position with four tricks to play:

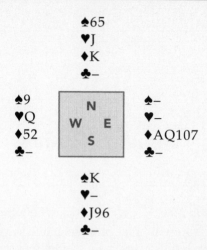

♠65
♥J
♦K
♣—

♠9   ♠—
♥Q   ♥—
♦52   ♦AQ107
♣—   ♣—

♠K
♥—
♦J96
♣—

Hamman played a diamond to the king, and East was stuck. If he played the ♦Q, Hamman would ruff in dummy, then play a spade to his king, pulling the last trump, and would have the good ♦J for his tenth trick. If East exited with a low diamond after winning the ace, Hamman would play the ♦J, pull the last trump and enjoy the ♠6 as his tenth trick. Hamman had brought home a contract that seemed hopeless even after the defensive error.

Even when things look hopeless, if you keep trying and do your best, often you will find that you have overcome your obstacles to success. Fate has a way of rewarding those with the most determination.

Chapter 13

Numbers to Know

You will face many situations in bridge play for which no easy answer presents itself. You will often play detective in your search for the best way to make your contract, but sometimes the information will not be sufficient to present you with one line of play significantly better than another. You will make some decisions intuitively. In others, you will rely on the odds. It will help you in this task to learn a few basic percentages.

> **Principle 85: Understand that percentages do not provide guarantees.**

Here's a common situation. You need one extra trick in a side suit to make your contract. You have the ♣AQ in dummy opposite a singleton in your hand. Your other suit is ♦AKQ5 in your hand opposite ♦632 in dummy. If diamonds split 3-3, your 5 will take the extra trick you need.

Ordinarily, you would try cashing the ♦AKQ first to see if you get a favorable split. If not, you will take the finesse in clubs. The problem you face now is that your left-hand opponent has made you decide right away—he has led a club. If you go up with the ace, that's the end of the finesse. You will have to rely on a 3-3 split in diamonds. The opponents have provided no information in the bidding and you have not had a chance to discover anything more in the play. What do you do?

Going strictly by the odds, your better play is to finesse. Half the time the ♣K will be on your left; the other half it will be on your right. The diamond suit is a different matter, however. When you are missing six cards in a suit, the chances that the suit will split 3-3 are 31.75 percent, compared to 46.88 percent for a 4-2 split, not to mention 5-1 and 6-0 breaks. Remember, you have not had a chance to find out information about distribution. So it's 50 percent for the club finesse versus about 32 percent for a favorable split in diamonds. That's a big difference.

In the long run, if you play percentages such as these you will come out ahead, but that's assuming you have no other information to go by. For example, if your left-hand opponent had passed originally and had already shown up with, say the ♠AKQ, you would reject the club finesse because it could not possibly work (West would have opened the bidding with that many high-card points).

The main thing to remember is not to beat yourself up if, in the example situation, you take the finesse, losing to the king, and find afterward that the diamond suit was 3-3 after all. You won't get every one of these right. It was astute of your opponent to make you guess before having a chance to try the diamond play.

♣ ♦ ♥ ♠

Unless you are an actuary, be careful about letting numbers rule your world.

➤ Principle 86: Learn basic percentages.

You have a lot to learn as an aspiring bridge player, and certain elementary percentages should be among them. You should not, however, clog your mind trying to remember all the numbers available to you. There are many sources of information about suit splits and odds regarding distributions. You will be well served if you know basics, such as the most common distributional patterns. If you know most of an opponent's hand and you are trying to figure out whether he or his partner holds four of a particular suit, it might be helpful to know the most common hand pattern is 4-4-3-2.

The previous principle touched on the odds regarding finesses. All things being equal, finessing give you a 50 percent chance of succeeding. Odds change as you go along, however, and you uncover information. For example, if you are looking for a queen and determine that one opponent has four cards in that suit and the other has two, the queen is twice as likely to be in the hand with four cards. That doesn't mean it will be, but it is more likely.

Make it your business to learn elementary percentages, but don't go overboard. If you clutter your mind with too much, it will be that much harder to do the real work of playing bridge—thinking.

♣ ♦ ♥ ♠

*Trying to take on too much information at the start
of a project can cloud your vision of your overall goal.*

▷ Principle 87: Know when to ignore percentages.

You don't play bridge in a vacuum—and you don't play bridge like an automaton. Part of successful bridge play is knowing your opponents, cultivating that nebulous quality known as "table feel," and backing your judgment.

The following deal was play in the world championships in Taipei in 1971 by Bobby Wolff, one of the all-time great players:

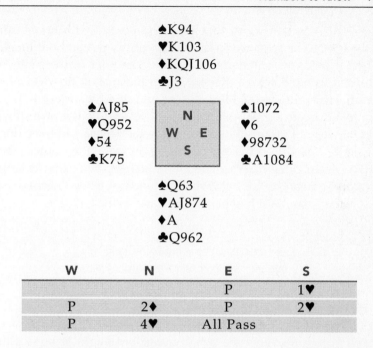

♠K94
♥K103
♦KQJ106
♣J3

♠AJ85
♥Q952
♦54
♣K75

♠1072
♥6
♦98732
♣A1084

♠Q63
♥AJ874
♦A
♣Q962

W	N	E	S
		P	1♥
P	2♦	P	2♥
P	4♥	All Pass	

The players at the table were a very strong French pair, facing Wolff (South) and the late Jim Jacoby.

West started off with a club to East's ace. A spade was returned to West's ace and he quickly cashed the ♣K. At trick four, West played another spade to Wolff's queen. Stopping to think about the situation, Wolff wondered why West was so anxious to take the ♣K. He finally decided that West was pretty sure he was going to take a trump trick.

Backing his judgment, Wolff played the ♥J from his hand at trick five. This was covered by West, another play that caused a blip on Wolff's internal radar screen. It would be unusual for a player to help declarer out in such a way. Usually in this situation declarer is trying to flush out the queen, and a champion-caliber player would not be likely to be so helpful without a reason.

Wolff was convinced that West had started with four hearts to the Q-9, so he returned to his hand with the ♦A and ran the ♥7. When it held, he was home. He played another heart to the 10, returned to hand with a diamond ruff and picked up West's last trump. He could use the ♠K to enter dummy, which was good.

Wolff made a great play based on his intuition. It also shows that he was not afraid to look foolish, which he would have done if East had produced the ♥Q or the ♥9. In fact, at the other table, South (also playing in 4♥) made the standard play of a heart to the king and a heart to the jack, which would have been necessary if East rather than West had held four hearts to the Q-9.

♣ ♦ ♥ ♠

You can't make every decision by intuition,
but "gut feel" can be surprisingly accurate.

▷ Principle 88: Know the scoring.

At times you will have to make decisions about whether to sacrifice. If you don't know the penalty your bid might bring—or the value of the contract over which you are saving—you may misjudge. It doesn't take long to familiarize yourself with the scores: four down, not vulnerable is 800 (minus 100 for the first undertrick, minus 200 for the second and third and minus 300 for all subsequent undertricks). It's different if you are vulnerable: minus 200 for the first undertrick and minus 300 for all subsequent undertricks.

It is worth noting that Jeff Meckstroth, one of the world's great players, is responsible for the three steps in the nonvulnerable undertrick scheme. In a world championship, his vulnerable opponents bid to 7♥. With a long spade suit and little else, Meckstroth bid 7♠ out of the blue. He was doubled and went down 9 tricks for minus 1700, hardly enough to compensate the opponents for their vulnerable grand slam bonus of 2210. One observer, a person of influence regarding the laws, pushed through the scoring change. Today, the same result would be minus 2300.

♣ ♦ ♥ ♠

You need the right information to make good decisions under pressure.

➤ Principle 89: Learn the basic "rules."

When it comes to rules, bridge has plenty—and there are just as many exceptions. Some "rules" are not commands, however. They are aids to bidding and play. One of the most-used rules is the Rule of 11, with which all but the rankest beginner is familiar.

Lately, the Rule of 20 has achieved some currency. That is the guideline for helping you to determine, in borderline cases, whether to open the bidding.

Some lesser-known rules are helpful, so long as you discuss them with your partner. One in particular is the Rule of 8, which is used in competitive situations, mostly when you are overcalling after a weak two-bid. When the person to your right opens 2♦, 2♥, or 2♠, your life becomes more difficult. You might have a hand you were considering for an opening bid, but having to start at the two or three level is daunting. Perhaps your suit is not so good, or is only five cards in length.

If you employ the Rule of 8, you will assume your partner has a semi-useful 8 high-card points, which is what he will have on average. This gives you a measure of safety you might not feel if the Rule of 8 is not part of your thinking. Of course, sometimes partner will have a very weak hand and you might suffer a big set, but if you wait until you have the perfect hand to bid after the opponents jam your auction, you will be a loser in the long run.

It's important to go over the Rule of 8 with your partner because he must use it as well. If your right-hand opponent opens 2♥ and you bid 2♠, partner's natural tendency with a modest hand and spade support will be to raise. He must remember, however, to remain silent unless he has at least a king better than the 8 HCP you were expecting from him. In other words, you have already bid his first 8 HCP, so he must have something extra—four or more trumps, a singleton or void, 10 or 11 HCP—to make a move.

These are a few of the rules you can use to make your life easier. Remember that they are not rules that give you commands. They are your servants if you use them correctly.

There is at least a grain of truth in even the most well-worn platitude.

> **Principle 90: Take advantage of what the opponents "tell" you.**
Percentage plays will always be in your mind, but there are many occasions when the opponents give you enough information that you do not need to rely on mathematics to land your contract.

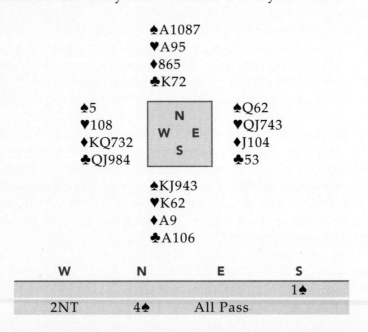

	♠A1087	
	♥A95	
	♦865	
	♣K72	
♠5	N	♠Q62
♥108	W E	♥QJ743
♦KQ732	S	♦J104
♣QJ984		♣53
	♠KJ943	
	♥K62	
	♦A9	
	♣A106	

W	N	E	S
			1♠
2NT	4♠	All Pass	

You are South and open 1♠. West's 2NT bid shows a hand with at least five cards in each minor. It is a blocking bid, but it can also be constructive. If East has a lot of one of the minors, it's possible East-West can make something. The 2NT bid creates a problem for North, who has a pretty good hand and was planning to make a limit raise (10–11 high-card points, four or more trumps) until West threw a spanner into the works. The problem is that a bid of 3♠ by North would be made on much less of a hand, and South won't know whether it's a 6-point hand or something closer to the actual hand. Unless North-South have a special agreement about how to cope with the 2NT bid in this situation, it's best for North to go ahead and jump to game.

Your problem is how to make it.

West leads the ♦K and you play low on the first trick as East plays the ♦J, which is either a singleton or shows possession of the 10 (much more likely). West continues with a low diamond to your ace (East does not play the 10—he knows you have the bare ace left). You have lost a trick in diamonds and you are likely to have losers in clubs and hearts as well. You must bring in the spade suit for no losers. How do you play the suit? Taken in isolation, your best play is to cash the ace and king. It's 58 percent that the queen will drop. This is not an isolated case, however. Because ten of West's cards are known, the odds now favor East holding the ♠Q. Of course, there is no law that says West can't have a singleton heart and a doubleton ♠Q, so you had better do a little detective work.

At trick three, play the ♥K. Assuming all follow, play another heart. If West started with a singleton and he ruffs, he is ruffing your loser. You will end up losing one diamond, one spade (a ruff), and one club but no hearts. If West follows to the second heart, win the ace. You now know all but one of West's cards. It is a simple matter to cash the ♠A, and if West follows, take the marked finesse against East's queen. The 58 percent play for the drop just became the 100 percent play for the finesse.

A small digression is in order. West's bid of 2NT is one that most players would make. In most cases, it would be the correct decision. There are times, however, when using the 2NT convention does more harm to your side than good. West's minor suits are not terribly weak, but they are not exactly robust, either. If East-West were vulnerable, playing against nonvulnerable opponents, 2NT would be a dubious overcall. It still might work out, but there would be a serious danger of calamity as well. If North is stacked in one or both minors, East will almost certainly end up playing a doubled contract at the three level.

The bottom line here is that at unfavorable vulnerability, there is little chance that your side will be able to outbid the opponents, so it is folly to make a bid that is so descriptive. To bid 2NT with no chance to buy the contract would be giving the opponents a free road map to the play. Before you make such a dubious overcall, ask yourself whether there is sufficient upside to take the risk.

Don't tell your secrets without a very good reason to do so.

Chapter 14

Protect Your Assets

If you remember that you need tricks to make your contracts in bridge, you will appreciate the importance of protecting the high cards that will produce those tricks. You will try to position these cards in such a way that the opponents cannot attack them to good effect. It is not always possible to establish foolproof protection, but you should be ever mindful of opportunities.

▷ Principle 91: Keep protection in mind when you open the bidding.
As you hone your bidding skills, you will be more likely to make decisions that pay off for you in safe—or at least safer—contracts and extra tricks.

♠AQ　　♥AQ73　　♦KJ832　　♣94

Purists would describe this hand as "off-shape" for a 1NT opener because it does not fit the profile of a "balanced" hand—4-3-3-3, 4-4-3-2, or 5-3-3-2 distribution. The one card out of place would be enough for some to start with 1♦.

Most experienced players would begin with 1NT despite the slight flaw for no-trump. The reason is the holdings in the majors.

If you open 1♦ with this hand and partner bids 1NT, you will certainly raise to 2NT. Partner may or may not bid the game, but putting your hand down as dummy—meaning the opening lead is going *through* your hand rather than *up to* it—could lead to serious trouble.

On the other hand, a spade lead into your A-Q would not be troubling in the least. There would be almost no chance that you would go down.

*Avoid the potential dangers you can see, as there
will be plenty more challenges that cannot be foreseen.*

▷ Principle 92: Steer the contract to the correct side when you can.
The opening bid will not be your only opportunity to "right-side" the contract. You will have chances even after the auction begins, and you should always be mindful of the opportunities to protect your holdings.

♠A76   ♥AK   ♦QJ9875   ♣K10

W	N	E	S
			1♦
P	1♥	1♠	?

Your partner's response to your opener makes you optimistic that your side may have game, and it's probably 3NT, a contract that requires only nine tricks, two fewer than game in a minor. Your ♠A is a stopper, but you will feel better about a no-trump contract if you have more than one. Partner might well have something in spades, but if you bid 3♦ (the book bid with your hand), he might not realize its worth.

♠Q5   ♥QJ107   ♦K106   ♣J543

With this hand after your 3♦ bid, partner will realize you have the high cards and/or shape for game, but with only two spades he does not have a stopper. The worst thing that could happen would be for your partner to bid 3♠ over your 3♦, asking if you have a spade stopper. Now the contract will be played from the wrong side, with tragic results for you.

♠Q5
♥QJ107
♦K106
♣J543

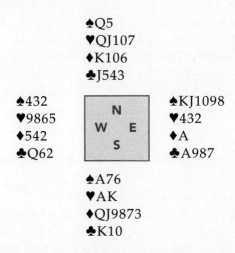

♠432	♠KJ1098
♥9865	♥432
♦542	♦A
♣Q62	♣A987

♠A76
♥AK
♦QJ9873
♣K10

You can see that if you play 3NT, West will lead a spade through dummy's queen, and no matter what you do, East will sooner or later have four spade tricks to cash along with two aces. Dummy's ♠Q is trapped.

Now look what happens when North plays 3NT. If East leads a spade, North will simply play low from dummy and his queen will win. He will then be able to knock out the ♦A and easily get home with eleven tricks (five diamonds, four hearts, and two spades). If East chooses not to lead a spade, your partner will have time to knock out the ♦A and make the game in comfort. The most testing lead would be a low club by East, but North will realize that if West has the ♣A, East most certainly will have the ♦A—and after West wins the ♦A he will push a spade through the queen, leading to defeat of the contract. So North will have no choice but to hope East has the ace. He will make the correct play in clubs—the king.

So, how do you steer the contract to the North hand?

You could start with a cuebid of 2♠. Partner will understand that you are asking for a stopper in spades, so he will deny a full stopper by bidding 3♣. When you cuebid again with 3♠, North will realize you need only a partial stopper, a doubleton queen, tripleton jack, or 4 to the 10. North will then bid 3NT and you will have your game.

Getting North to play the contract works when he has a doubleton queen and you have 3 to the ace no matter who has the king. Even if West wins the king after East leads the suit, the queen is now a trick and your side has a double stopper in spades.

♣ ♦ ♥ ♠

If you don't take care of yourself or your best assets, no one will.

➤ Principle 93: Remember the role of the ace.

Aces are great as quick tricks—you can win a trick with one immediately if you want. With a holding such as QJ10, unless the other hand has the ace or king, you will need to lead the suit twice to come up with a trick.

In general, aces are better for suit contracts, although there is no denying their value in no-trump play as well, especially when holding up one or two rounds is necessary for success.

You should also be aware of the combination where it is vital for the lead to come up to the hand with a doubleton ace, an exception to the principle discussed previously.

Consider this combination: A9 opposite J108. Now consider that the opponents are leading this suit. If the ace is led up to—say you hold the closed hand with A9 and the J108 are in dummy—you are guaranteed two tricks in the suit. Perhaps more important, you are assured of two stoppers.

It's a completely different story if the A9 are in dummy and the J108 are in your hand and the lead is coming from your left. If you play low and the king or queen wins, you will take only one trick. The suit will be returned, but the other honor will not be played when there is a bare ace left for all to see. If the opponents get in again, they will cash tricks in that suit and you will not be able to prevent it.

♣ ♦ ♥ ♠

The best, most modern tools you can find are worthless if not used correctly.

▷ Principle 94: Know when too many stoppers is a danger sign.

Some hands lend themselves more to suit contracts than to no-trump, but there will be danger signs to warn you away from the suit contract and you must train yourself to recognize them.

One situation easy to recognize is when you hold three or four cards in a suit opened on your left—and your partner overcalls 1NT. Your partner likely has three or four of the suit as well, and if you play in a suit contract, there is a very real possibility that the opening bidder's partner will get one or more ruffs in that suit.

If partner plays in no-trump, there will be no ruffs and it's likely he has spades stopped at least twice, perhaps three times. He will have ample time to develop needed tricks.

♣ ♦ ♥ ♠

Things are not always as they seem. You will be better
off if you make it a practice to look beneath the surface.

▷ Principle 95: Keep your honors safe during play.

The opening lead has been made and you have formulated your plan to fulfill your contract. There will be many occasions when you have options as to how to go about this task. If possible, you should choose the option that protects your assets from attack.

♠A543
♥A542
♦63
♣AJ7

```
    N

    S
```

♠K2
♥K83
♦KQ4
♣K10985

You are South playing 3NT. West leads the ♦J, and East plays the 2. You win the ♦Q. This contract cannot be defeated, but only if you take care.

You need the club suit, but not all five of them, and you can obviously finesse for the queen through either opponent's hand. If you manage to find the queen, you will make an overtrick.

The possibility of an overtrick should be the farthest thing from your mind, however, and you must take the line of play that guarantees your contract. Even in a pair game, where overtricks can be so important, it is best to play safe.

How do you do that? After winning the opening lead in your hand, simply play a club to dummy's ace and run the ♣J. You don't mind if it loses because you will still have four clubs, one diamond, and two tricks in each of the majors for your nine.

The danger in finessing against West for the ♣Q is that if you lose the lead to East, a diamond will certainly be returned, and your contract may well be sunk. Remember that West led the ♦J, which he would do from a holding of AJ10, and East played the 2, indicating that he has nothing in diamonds. That makes it likely that West has just the holding you fear, and if he started with five or six diamonds, your contract will be toast. A diamond return would go right through your K4 and you would be down. If the ♣Q is with East, you will have your overtrick, but no matter what, if you play correctly you will make your contract.

There are other ways to try to protect cards in one hand or the other. Say you hold ♣AQ10874 opposite ♣J932 and receive an opening lead similar to the one in the previous example. You cannot afford to let your right-hand opponent in. You must develop the club suit to make your contract, but you don't need six club tricks. Five will do.

The right way to play the club suit in this case is to lead low and, if West follows low, play the ace. There are only three clubs out, and what you can't afford is to lose to a singleton king on your right. If your left-hand opponent has the king, it's okay. He will win the next trick, but he will not be able to hurt you.

When opportunity knocks, make sure you are in a position to take advantage.

Chapter 15

Counting—
Unlocking the Door to Your Tricks

If you were to ask 100 expert players what they consider essential to success at bridge, 100 of them would tell you that it's counting. To be successful, you must learn to make this aspect of your game as routine as picking up your hand to begin play. When you acquire the habit of counting every hand, plays you would have considered beyond your ability will seem easy. You will win the respect of people you looked up to. They will ask you to play. You will have arrived.

➤ Principle 96: Do not be intimidated by the task of counting.

There is no doubt that learning to count is hard work at first, particularly if you have not been doing it, but consider how often during a typical day counting is an almost automatic part of your routine. You count out change when you buy a cup of coffee; you count the minutes to your next break or to the end of the workday. You are counting when you measure ingredients for a meal you are cooking. With all of these, you don't give it a second thought.

Now consider bridge. You count your high-card points when you pick up your hand. If your count of HCP indicates that you should open, you count the cards in the four suits to determine which suit you will start with. When partner opens, you count up your points and what he has indicated to determine whether to play game or slam or just a part score. You're doing a lot of counting already without having to think about doing it. Yes, experts do it better than you do, but that doesn't mean you can't do it, too. It's all a matter of practice and determination. As long as you understand how important counting is in your development as a player, you will be patient with yourself and the process. The rewards will be well worth the effort.

A journey of a thousand miles begins with a single step.

> **Principle 97: Understand the wonders of bridge as a "counter."**
Once you acquire the habit of counting a bridge hand, your confidence will soar. A bridge hand will take on an entirely new look. You will know as a defender that partner or declarer has certain cards, and you will know what to do about it. You will be viewed as a dangerous opponent.

W	N	E	S
1NT	P	2♣	P
2♠	P	3♠	P
4♠	All Pass		

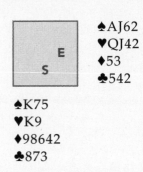

```
                          ♠AJ62
                          ♥QJ42
                  E       ♦53
                  S       ♣542


        ♠K75
        ♥K9
        ♦98642
        ♣873
```

West's 1NT showed 15–17 HCP, and his acceptance of the invitation to game indicates he is at the top of the range. Your partner starts with the ♦K, taken by West with the ace. Next, West plays the top three clubs—AKQ—and discards dummy's losing diamond. At trick six, West plays the ♠Q, which runs to your king. Now what?

If you have been counting, you will know what to do.

So far, you have seen the ♦A and the ♣AKQ, plus the ♠Q. How many high-card points is that? That's right—15. It is possible for West to have the ♥A? Only if he has lied about his opening bid. With the ♥A, West would have 19 HCP, 20 if he has the ♣J. No one opens 1NT with 19 or 20 HCP.

Partner has the ♥A, so it's an easy move for you to play the ♥K and a heart to partner's ace so that he can play another heart for you to ruff. That's down one. West didn't have any choice about his line of play. If he took the spade finesse at trick two, he would have lost that trick plus a diamond and the two top hearts. West would have preferred not to give you so much information, but he was a bit unlucky that you were playing against him—*and* you had a doubleton heart. The full deal follows:

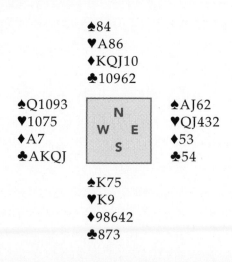

```
              ♠84
              ♥A86
              ♦KQJ10
              ♣10962
♠Q1093                        ♠AJ62
♥1075         N               ♥QJ432
♦A7        W     E            ♦53
♣AKQJ         S               ♣54
              ♠K75
              ♥K9
              ♦98642
              ♣873
```

♣ ♦ ♥ ♠

*You will appreciate the achievement of a goal
all the more if it took hard work on your part.*

▷ Principle 98: Understand why counting is important.

You have just seen in the previous principle how exciting it can be to make a play that would have been very difficult without the practice of counting. While some players might look in awe as you cash your ♥K and get a ruff, you will consider it routine.

While it's fun to make the kinds of plays that attract attention, there is a stronger motivation for acquiring this invaluable skill.

You are learning to count, not to show off, but to avoid making very silly mistakes.

If you neglect counting as part of your bridge training, you will make innumerable errors simply because you don't know what's going on. Time and again, you will find yourself at a crossroads in a bridge deal, knowing that the next play you make will be crucial to the outcome—and you won't have any idea what to do. That feeling stays with you and saps your confidence.

Counting helps you fight your way out of the fog.

♣ ♦ ♥ ♠

*The brain needs exercise the same as the body's muscles.
Give your little gray cells a regular workout.*

▷ Principle 99: Learn what to count.

You are not without resources when it comes to counting. For one thing, you have an opportunity to see dummy on every deal you play. You can take inferences about hands from what you see on display. Right away, you are looking at half of the cards. That makes a fine start to your task of mentally building the other two hands.

For example, when you are defending against a contract that started with a 1NT bid by an opponent, make it your habit to add your high-card points to what you can see in dummy. You will then know the range of high-card points that your partner can have. This information can be of critical importance later in the deal.

For example, suppose your right-hand opponent has opened 1NT and lands in a contract of 3NT. Your hand contains 10 HCP, and when dummy comes down, it does, too. You can see 20 HCP, and declarer has 15–17, so your partner can have at most 5 HCP, but he might have only 3 HCP. You may get in at a point where your partner has played an ace. If so, you know the most he can have left is a jack. Knowing this may keep you from making a play based on a hope that partner has something more. If you are counting and paying attention, that's a mistake you won't make.

It is also important to keep track of the distribution as the play unfolds. The bidding will almost always help you get started on your count of a deal. If one of your opponents has bid two suits, he will generally have at least nine cards in those two suits. That information should pop into your head automatically, and it will when you become a counter.

W	N	E	S
1♠	P	1NT	P
2♥	P	P	3♣
All Pass			

♠K109
♥Q964
♦A103
♣1072

N
S

♠543
♥8
♦K982
♣AK854

West starts with the ♠Q, which you cover. East wins the ♠A, returns a spade to West's jack and takes a spade ruff. Back comes a low heart to West's ace, and the ♥J is continued. You ruff and assess the situation. You would have been better off, as it happens, balancing with 2NT. As a passed hand, this could not be natural. Not only that, the opponents have bid the other two suits, so 2NT would have to say to partner, "Pick a minor."

That is neither here nor there. You must do your best to make this contract because it is clear that West was going to have trouble making his heart contract with the bad split in hearts. You start by cashing the ♣A and ♣K in your hand, and you are gratified to see both opponents following suit, West with the 3 and queen and East with the 9 and jack. East has ruffed with a natural trump trick, which is good for your side.

It is now time to tackle diamonds, and you need some luck. You play a low diamond from hand, and the queen pops up from the West hand. What do you think about that?

You have the spots to finesse against East's theoretical ♦J, but should you do it?

Not if you have been counting. West has shown up with five spades and four hearts—he certainly would have bid more if he had been 5-5 in the majors. You have seen West's only two clubs, so he must have started with two diamonds, and unless West has lost his mind and played the ♦Q from Q-x, he is sitting there hoping you weren't paying attention and are planning to finesse.

You have counted West's hand and drawn your inferences, so there's no fooling you this time. You play a diamond to the king, dropping West's jack, and claim. The full deal follows:

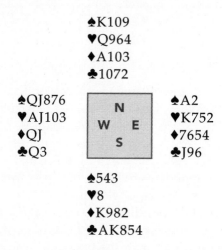

Did you note that West could have defeated you by continuing with a fourth round of spades? If he does, East can ruff with the jack or 9, promoting his partner's queen to the setting trick.

The key to good decision-making is having sufficient, accurate information.

> **Principle 100: Don't forget to count tricks, too.**

You have been counting high cards and distribution so far. Be sure you count tricks as well—your own and those of the opponents.

Start with your own tricks. When you are the declarer, you should make it an automatic process to count the number of tricks you have as soon as the dummy comes down. Compare that to the number of tricks you need. If the two numbers are the same, you can start considering how you might gain some overtricks. Usually, however, you will be short of your goal. You can't know where you need to go, however, if you don't know where you are.

♠Q6542
♥K106
♦A86
♣43

N
S

♠A3
♥AQ984
♦K54
♣A95

W	N	E	S
			1♥
P	2♥	P	4♥
All Pass			

West leads the ♦Q, which you take in hand. That five-card spade suit in dummy looks good. If West has the ♠K, you can draw trumps and play the ♠A and another spade. West may win the ♠K, but the queen will provide a parking place for your losing diamond, and if spades go 3-3, you can use the other two to discard your losing clubs.

If you start this hand by counting your top tricks, however, you may come up with a better plan. You have five heart tricks, assuming the suit splits reasonably. You have two diamond tricks (the ace and king) plus two other tricks in the black aces. That's nine tricks. Your objective is ten. If things don't work out in spades as you hope, that suit may produce only one trick, and the club suit is strictly limited to one.

Instead of relying on West to hold the ♠K, a much better play is to organize a club ruff in dummy. Draw no trumps. At trick two, play the ♣A and a low club from hand. Now, even if the suit splits 6-2 with the doubleton in the East hand, you will still survive if East does not have the ♥J.

That club ruff in the dummy is your tenth trick. You found this play because you counted your tricks as soon as your partner put down the dummy.

It is equally important to count tricks when you are a defender. It is not as easy because often the declarer will hide his assets to make your job more difficult. Inferences from the bidding and play will aid you, however, and if you have gained the lead and can reasonably conclude that declarer has the tricks he needs for his contract, you can base your next play on whatever chance, even a slim one, you might have to prevail.

Do not be lazy in your decision-making. Take the steps you need to get complete information before you act.

➤ Principle 101: Practice counting to get better at it.
There are exercises you can do to help make counting a comfortable part of your bridge-playing regimen.

One such exercise is to repeat, over and over, various distributions. Say them to yourself; go over them when your head hits the pillow at bedtime. Get someone to practice with you. One of you will say, "Five, four, three . . ." and the other will fill in the missing part: "One." Again, "Six, three, two . . ." Partner answers: "Two."

Practice the common shapes: 4-4-3-2, 5-4-2-2, 5-4-3-1, 6-3-2-2, 6-3-3-1, 4-4-4-1, 7-2-2-2. As you ingrain them in your subconscious mind, the information will be available to you without your having to think about it.

When one of your opponents opens 1♠ and rebids 2♥, your mind will say "Five-four in the majors." It will leave open whether the other four cards are 2-2, 3-1, or 4-0. If declarer shows up with a void in one of the other suits, you will know his exact distribution, within a card or two (he might have six spades and four hearts).

As a defender, you should also make it your practice when dummy comes down to add your points to dummy's and then add in declarer's likely points. That way, you will always have an approximation of partner's high-card strength.

When declarer's hand becomes an open book, so does your partner's.

Even if you have to start out slowly, counting only one suit at a time, don't let up. It may seem that you are making slow progress, but if you keep at it and keep counting, one day you will realize that you don't have to work at it so hard. It has become an automatic action. You are free to spend your mental energy on other aspects of declarer play and defense.

What does not come naturally can be learned through hard work.

> **Principle 102: Never underestimate the help you can get from your opponents.**

Bidding is a language. It's the way partners tell each other about their hands. This is a good thing and a bad thing, depending on your point of view.

The rules of bridge require that you disclose your bidding systems and that you explain any bids if asked. This applies mainly to special agreements and unusual conventions, but the point is that when you are "speaking" to your partner, the opponents are listening.

Astute opponents really hear the bidding and they make use of the information that is being tossed about the table.

Some bidding conventions convey a lot of information, so it's wise to be careful about using them. Bids that show two long suits are especially informative. The Unusual No-trump is a good example. If you open one of a major and the next person bids 2NT, that is not a strong bid—it shows at least ten cards in the minors. Already, everyone at the table knows the hand within three cards.

High-level preemptive bids also provide a lot of information. If your opponent opens 3♣ and you subsequently win the auction, you already know a tremendous amount about that 3♣ hand. You need play only six cards to know the 3♣ bidder's entire hand—and when you know that hand, you will know his partner's hand as well.

What you need to know for success is all around you,
but you won't be able to use it if you're not aware.

> **Principle 103: When there's only one shot, take it.**

A big part of success in bridge is the ability to analyze your situation. There will be many times when you take what you feel is the only shot, and then you find out in the postgame analysis that there were a couple of other chances. Don't be discouraged if your analytical skills aren't as good as you would like them to be. It's part of the fascination of bridge that there are so many things to learn. While some situations may be murky, there will be easily identifiable "only chances."

♠AQ54
♥Q96
♦A4
♣J1072

	N	
	S	

♠J10987
♥J107
♦KQJ5
♣A

W	N	E	S
P	1♣	P	1♠
P	2♠	P	4♠
All Pass			

West starts with the ♥K, then the ♥A, East playing the ♥8 and ♥2, indicating a doubleton. West continues with the ♥3 (a low card showing suit-preference for clubs) and East ruffs. The ♣9 comes back and you win the ace as West plays a high club, further evidence that he holds the ♣K.

The normal play in spades is to finesse against the king with West, but this is a play that cannot succeed. If you have been paying attention, you will know that West cannot have the ♠K. West has shown up with the top two hearts, and there are strong indications he holds the ♣K as well.

That's 10 high-card points. If he had the ♠K, that would be 13 HCP—but he passed as dealer. Your only shot—and this one is crystal clear—is that East started with only two spades (he used one earlier to ruff, remember). You must play a spade to the ace in dummy and hope the king comes tumbling down. It is certainly futile to finesse against West for a card he cannot hold.

It's possible that West is playing a deep and devious game to make you believe he has the ♣K when he really doesn't. In general, players tend to signal honestly to keep their partners happy.

Sometimes there's nothing to do but swing for the fences.
If you strike out, at least you know you gave it your best shot.

Chapter 16

Be a Squeezer

Among the fascinations of bridge is the array of advanced plays available to true students of the game. The squeeze is a fine example.
There are so many variations that it boggles the mind, from simple
squeezes to exotic-sounding plays such as the backwash squeeze
or the crisscross squeeze. In general, it is not necessary to master
the super-advanced plays—mainly because they come up so infre-
quently—but it will behoove you to study enough to recognize the
chance for a squeeze or endplay when it arises. Just don't overdo it.

➤ **Principle 104: Know your basics first.**
There is no short supply of reading material if you are truly interested in learning advanced plays, but there is a danger in putting
too much emphasis on this area of your game early on.

It is easy to become enamored of squeezes and endplays to the
point where you are trying to execute some such play on practically every hand you encounter. This can lead to countless poor
results, which can be discouraging.

The fact is that some advanced plays—squeezes included—
come up spontaneously. You may not even realize it the first time
you squeeze an opponent for an extra trick. The first time you do it
on purpose, it will be a significant point in your development, but
don't try to rush it.

You should strive to have a solid foundation in the basics of card play. Let good technique be your goal in the early stages of your development. When basic technique is mastered, you will be more relaxed and more likely to uncover the possibilities for advanced plays. The squeezes, endplays, and trump coups will come in time.

You must crawl before you can walk.

> **Principle 105: Familiarize yourself with advanced techniques.**
You don't want to spend your bridge life looking for squeezes or endplays, but it will help you if you figure out the basics of some of these exotic-sounding plays.

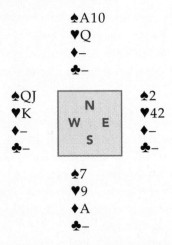

South needs the rest of the tricks, but West seems to have a spade stopper—and his ♥K is bigger than dummy's queen. When South plays the ♦A, West is finished. If he discards the ♥K, dummy's queen will be good. If West discards a spade, dummy's ♠10 will be good. West is squeezed on the play of the diamond.

That is an illustration of the mechanics of the squeeze. It will be up to you, as the British say, to suss out the situations in which squeezes will work. Be aware that when a squeeze is executed, it won't always be with kings, queens, and jacks. More often it will be with much lower cards. If the play calls for a squeeze and it's working, it doesn't matter, of course, whether you squeeze someone out of an 8 or an ace.

You will have a better chance of high-level achievement
if you master the basics of your discipline first.

▷ Principle 106: Know the one-trick rule.

The first thing to remember about the squeeze is that, with rare exceptions, the play will produce only one extra trick.

That's because of the way the squeeze operates. The victim of the squeeze must find a discard from his hand at a time when whatever he does promotes a trick in your hand or dummy's. Cards that the squeeze victim needs to hold on to are characterized as "busy" cards, as opposed to "idle" cards, which can be discarded without discomfort. The squeeze victim must be down to all busy cards such as the ♠QJ and the ♥K in the example in the previous principle. Try that end position by giving each hand one extra card—in any suit. When South plays the ♦A, West can let go of whatever extra card he received because it would be an idle card. No squeeze operates because if South is to take the rest of the tricks, he would need two extras—he has only two top tricks in a four-card ending.

The bottom line is that there is no point in trying for a squeeze unless you are one—and only one—trick short of your goal. It all sounds complicated, but it really isn't. If you train yourself to count your tricks, you will readily size up your situation regarding squeeze possibilities. If you are in a ten-trick game and you have eight tricks, look somewhere else unless you have the chance to develop a ninth trick before the defenders can take four.

♣ ♦ ♥ ♠

No matter how good your technique is,
if it's applied to the wrong job it won't work.

➤ Principle 107: Learn to recognize the best chance for a squeeze.

There are certain key questions you can ask yourself if you are considering a squeeze as a way to make your contract. Start off with this question: How many tricks to do I have? Followed by: How many tricks do I need? If the answer is one, continue.

Even if the answer to the first two questions is not one, there may be a way to rectify the situation. In fact, there is a name for the process of losing a certain number of tricks to get to the point where all you need is one more. It's called rectifying the count. That is, if you need seven tricks and all you have is six, you have some chances, but you must have those six tricks with seven tricks remaining. If you're at the start of play, you have to lose a few tricks to get to the point of squeezing someone.

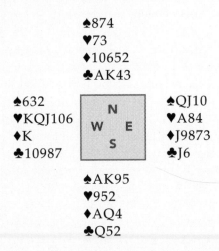

```
                    ♠874
                    ♥73
                    ♦10652
                    ♣AK43
  ♠632                              ♠QJ10
  ♥KQJ106         N                 ♥A84
  ♦K            W   E               ♦J9873
  ♣10987           S                ♣J6
                    ♠AK95
                    ♥952
                    ♦AQ4
                    ♣Q52
```

You are South and open 1NT, which is passed out. West starts with the ♥K, continuing with the ♥Q when East signals encouragement with the ♥8. The opponents cash five heart tricks. You discard two spades and a diamond from dummy and a spade and a diamond from your hand. East discards a low diamond and a low club.

After cashing the hearts, West exits with the ♣10. You win in dummy, noting the fall of the ♣J, and take the diamond finesse, losing to West's singleton king. On the return of the ♣9, you notice East starting to squirm. He eventually discards a diamond, his third play of that suit.

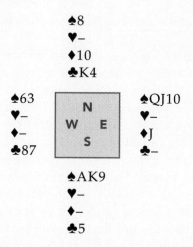

```
              ♠8
              ♥–
              ◆10
              ♣K4
  ♠63                    ♠QJ10
  ♥–        N            ♥–
  ◆–      W   E          ◆J
  ♣87       S            ♣–
              ♠AK9
              ♥–
              ◆–
              ♣5
```

You win the club return in hand, cash the ◆A (maybe West started with a doubleton K-J), and when you play your third club to dummy's king, East is in agony. What can East do? If he discards the ◆J, your 10 will be good, and if pitches a spade, your 9 will take the seventh trick. He is well and truly squeezed.

Note that there was a very important condition for this play to work. You had to be able to reach your hand, where the ♠9 was threatening East's spade suit. If you had no communication with the South hand from dummy, East could easily have discarded a spade and taken the last trick with the ♦J.

For that reason, West could have defeated you by playing a spade when he got in with the ♦K, disrupting your communications.

♣ ♦ ♥ ♠

Timing is often a critical factor in success—in business and in life.

➤ Principle 108: Beware of squeeze syndrome.

The first time you execute a squeeze on purpose—you almost certainly will have done it by accident a few times prior to that—it will be a thrill unlike any you have experienced in bridge to that point.

You will like the feeling that you are advancing—and you will appreciate the admiring glances of the players at the table when it happens. Just don't let it go to your head.

Yes, you have demonstrated that advanced techniques are within your grasp, but you will undo a lot of your progress if you play every hand for a squeeze, trying to duplicate the feat.

Squeezes come up at lot more often than many players think they do—but not as much as you would like after you experience it the first time. Show some discipline and patience. Take your squeeze for what it was: a good sign of your progress. You will have plenty of other chances, and you will enjoy them more if you are not straining to find squeezes ten times a session.

♣ ♦ ♥ ♠

Good things come to those who watch and wait.

➤ Principle 109: Don't worry about super-advanced plays.

Students of the game can find endless fascination in the study of truly esoteric end positions and endplays that might come up once in a millennium. Entire books have been written on the subject.

Fittingly, super-advanced plays have strange and arcane names—nonmaterial and entry-shifting squeezes, devil's coup, grand trump coup—the list goes on and on. Some of these are, in reality, not as complex as their names suggest, and some with colorful names—such as the Morton's fork coup—are really quite simple.

It's great to study some of these deals to see how wonderfully complex the game of bridge can be, but it's best to concentrate on mastery of the more common, if sometimes strangely named, plays that you will see on a regular basis.

♣ ♦ ♥ ♠

Using ordinary tools, you can still create something extraordinary.

▷ Principle 110: Sometimes a finesse is better.

It's likely that the finesse was the first "advanced" play you learned as a bridge infant. You have learned since, of course, to look for ways to improve on the roughly 50 percent chance of success when you do opt for that play.

In that sense, the simple finesse is viewed with contempt—or at least a healthy suspicion—by many players as they advance. There's a certain cachet to making a contract by executing a squeeze, the theory being that "anyone can take a finesse"—but it takes a good player to do it via a squeeze.

That's nothing more than a variation of the squeeze syndrome. Sometimes, like it or not, a finesse offers a better chance for the contract and you just have to suck it up and take it.

World champion Bobby Wolff once played in a grand slam and got the opening lead of a diamond. Dummy held the ♦AQ and Wolff had two low cards in his hand. Taking a finesse at trick one in a grand slam is about as scary a prospect as you will find, so Wolff had to think very carefully about what to do.

Wolff had twelve top tricks and some prospects for developing his thirteenth.

Wolff analyzed his situation, concluding that there were squeeze chances on the deal, but it would take an unlikely lie of the cards for any such play to materialize—certainly less than 50-50, which is what the diamond finesse represented. After long study, he finally put in the queen—and he was right! Furthermore, his analysis of the other chances was also correct. He had to take the finesse—risking going down at trick one—to make the contract.

Oftentimes, the solution to a problem is the simplest
and most obvious—if you just let yourself see it.

Chapter 17

On the Defensive

As you repeat the mantra that bridge is a game of tricks, you will realize that it's not just declarer who is out to take those elusive items. The defenders also have their eyes on a prize: enough tricks to defeat declarer's contract. Many players consider defense the most difficult aspect of the game, but for some it is easier. This is because of the information you can exchange with your partner when you are defending a contract. This communication, of course, is through the cards that you play, not the manner in which you play them. Your partner, if you have reasonable signaling methods, is helping you—and you are helping him.

> **Principle 111: Become a good opening leader.**

The defenders have the advantage on many deals because they get to take the opening shot. Getting the first punch in, so to speak, often is enough for the defense to prevail, but this is not a random activity. You will not be successful if you routinely start off with whatever card is closest to your thumb.

A good opening leader listens to the auction, sifting through information provided by bids that were made—and bids that were not made.

If you have no obvious lead yourself and are trying to "hit" partner's hand—in other words, find your partner's strength—be wary of leading a suit your partner could have overcalled at the one level.

W	N	E	S
1♦	P	1♥	P
2♦	P	2NT	P
3NT	All Pass		

♠765   ♥A9432   ♦76   ♣984

You have an awful hand to lead from, but partner might well have some high-card strength over there. East could be bidding 2NT on as little as 7 or 8 HCP. Your choices seem to be between spades and clubs. The latter is your best bet. With any strong holding in spades, your partner probably would have bid, even with a four-card suit. After all, he didn't have to bid more than 1♠ to enter the auction.

There will be many occasions when you can divine the opening lead from the auction. Even when you think there are no clues, they are there if you are listening. Even an auction such as 1NT—3NT by the opponents provides at minimum an inference: The opening bidder's partner did not use Stayman, so he probably doesn't have a four-card major. That can help you decide on your opening thrust.

A major part of solving a problem is identifying it.

> **Principle 112: Don't lead aces—except when it's right.**
You surely have heard the adage that aces are meant to take kings— and if you start with an ace at trick one you're unlikely to snag a king with it.

In general, it's bad policy to lead aces, and it applies equally to suit contracts and to no-trump. Banging down aces against suit contracts usually gives up at least one trick, sometimes more. Against no-trump, you might need that ace to cash the suit you hope to establish.

As with any of the seemingly hard and fast rules in bridge, there are many exceptions. It's a matter of keeping your ears open for the right time to lead that ace.

♠AQ54   ♥65   ♦J432   ♣QJ3

W	N	E	S
1♦	P	2♣	P
2♥	P	3♣	P
4♣	P	5♣	All Pass

This auction screams for a spade lead—and the chances that your partner has the ♠K are just about 100 percent. If East or West held that card, they would be playing 3NT, not 5♣. Almost no one plays in five of a minor if they have a viable alternative. If you don't start with the ♠A, East may be able to discard a spade loser or two and escape with eleven tricks. Even with the spade lead, you might not defeat 5♣, but at least you gave it a good shot.

Say your left-hand opponent opens 3♣, your partner passes and RHO bids 3NT. This is a the kind of auction where East may be taking a chance that he can run off nine tricks, using West's long clubs, before your side can get five tricks. Often East will have a suit that is wide open. He's hoping you lead a suit he has covered. If you have an ace, this is a good time to start with it. After you have a look at dummy, if continuing that suit does not seem profitable, the switch might be obvious. This is a race. You want your five tricks before declarer gets his nine.

♠A543   ♥K7   ♦QJ109   ♣543

Your right-hand opponent opens 1♥; his partner bids clubs. Soon they are in 6♥, using Blackwood along the way. The ♦Q is the "normal" opening lead, but the auction tells you it could be dangerous. It would be unusual for East to bid Blackwood with two or more quick losers in any suit. It would be equally odd for him to use Blackwood with a void in some suit—he wouldn't know whether his partner had the "right" ace if their side happened to be missing one.

There is an excellent chance that your ♥K will become a trick, and it's likely your ♠A will cash. Get it on the table before declarer throws his singleton spade away on one of dummy's high clubs.

♣ ♦ ♥ ♠

The more you learn, the more you realize that there truly are no absolutes.

> ➤ **Principle 113: Learn when a trump lead is best.**

A trump lead is often a passive lead—you don't want to lead away from your high cards for fear of blowing a trick or more. A trump lead can often be devastating to declarer's chances, however. As usual, the auction will help you find your way if you pay attention.

If, for example, you are on lead and are loaded in declarer's first suit, with two or three cards in the suit that is now trumps, get one on the table. Dummy will be short in the first suit, and declarer will use the trumps to ruff his losers—but only if you let him.

Another good indicator that a trump lead is called for is when declarer bids no-trump and dummy runs back to a suit. That's a clear indication dummy didn't think no-trump was a good idea—and that usually means there is some extreme shortage there. Again, a trump lead and continuation can cut down on ruffs in dummy.

Another fine time to lead trumps is when the opponents sacrifice at a high level. Frequently this action is based on a long suit and lots of trumps between the two hands. Also frequently, your side has the other three suits well under control and the opponents are hoping to make some of their trumps by ruffing. If you start leading trumps against them, it compresses their tricks and prevents those ruffs.

♣ ♦ ♥ ♠

You must know where you are going to make
the best decisions about how to get there.

➤ Principle 114: Keep your ear to the ground.

This has been said before, but it cannot be overemphasized—you must keep your head in the game and listen to the bidding, not just on opening lead but throughout the play. If you forget that declarer bid two suits and has shown up with three cards in another, it might slip past you that he almost certainly has only one card— maybe none—in the fourth suit.

If declarer bids 4NT, then 5NT, he is confirming that his side has all the aces (he wouldn't be trying for a grand slam if he was missing an ace). If this auction has taken place, don't go looking for an ace in partner's hand. If you're trying to decide between diamonds and clubs for your opening lead against a slam and you forget that partner didn't double a 5♦ response to Blackwood when he had the chance, you aren't taking advantage of all the information available.

Every bid tells a story—and some bids that are not made tell even more. You can't interpret them, however, if you aren't listening.

♣ ♦ ♥ ♠

Attention to detail can make the difference between success and failure.

➤ Principle 115: Less for you is more for your partner.

Get used to it: If you play long enough, you will have a lot of bad hands. In rubber bridge, this will probably mean losing. It doesn't have to be bad, however, if you are in a duplicate game. Remember, you get your score from comparisons, not the raw scores achieved on the deals. Plus 1100 can be a complete zero if everyone else holding your cards comes in with plus 1430 for bidding and making a vulnerable slam in a major.

When you hold bad cards, chances are you will find yourself on defense. If you think that's an opportunity for your brain to take a siesta, think again. You may have to try even harder.

One thing that will help is being aware that most of the time when you have a real dog of a hand, partner will be sitting across from you with some assets. In many cases, partner will be strong enough to bid or double to help you with your opening shot.

If your partner does not have a chance to indicate your lead, it will be up to you to try to "hit" your partner's values.

If you are on lead with a bad hand against a no-trump contract, it's usually folly to lead a long suit. Even if you can somehow establish the suit—pretty unlikely—how will you get in to cash your tricks?

♣ ♦ ♥ ♠

Life has a way of balancing things out. Your darkest days will often be followed by the brightest sunshine.

➤ **Principle 116: Know the difference between suits and no-trump.**
It is important to remember that, although your objective as a defender is to defeat the contract, the strategies can be markedly different.

Whereas there are only rare occasions when you would underlead an ace against a suit contract, it is commonplace when defending against a no-trump contract. The danger of under-leading an ace against a suit contract is that you might never win a trick with your ace. Against no-trump, you may need the ace as an entry back to your hand, in which case you don't want to release it too soon.

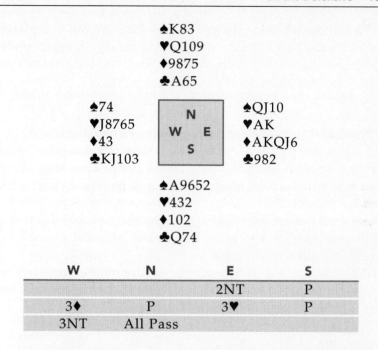

♠K83
♥Q109
♦9875
♣A65

♠74
♥J8765
♦43
♣KJ103

♠QJ10
♥AK
♦AKQJ6
♣982

♠A9652
♥432
♦102
♣Q74

W	N	E	S
		2NT	P
3♦	P	3♥	P
3NT	All Pass		

East's 2NT opener shows a hand with 20–21 HCP. West bids 3♦, a transfer to hearts, then gives East a choice of games by bidding 3NT. This is a common sequence in duplicate games and tournaments.

You start with your fourth-best spade and partner provides a pleasant surprise by winning with the king. East follows with the ♠10. North continues with the ♠8 and East plays the queen. It seems natural for you to win the queen with the ace and clear the suit, but that will be the end of the defense if you do. East will eventually have to play on clubs, and when partner comes in with the ♣A, he will have no spade to return. Declarer will make his contract with ease.

It's a different matter if you play low on the second round of spades. Doing so gives declarer the trick he is always going to win in spades, and it leaves your partner with a spade to play to your ace if and when he gets in again.

You not only underled your ace at the start, but you played low when you had a chance to take one of the opponent's honors.

♣ ♦ ♥ ♠

Be patient. A series of small advances will accomplish more than one big push.

> **Principle 117: In general, be aggressive on opening lead.**

You will acquire the habit of listening to the bidding to gather clues for your opening leads. As your "hearing" becomes more acute, your first thrust will become more accurate and more deadly. You will also know when it's best to pull in your horns and be passive. These situations are pretty easy to recognize: You have all or nearly all of your side's assets, but all in broken suits and tenaces you don't want to lead away from.

That said, it's usually best to be at least mildly aggressive on opening lead. Another way to put it is that it's best, when you can, to lead from "something" rather than nothing.

♠K1054   ♥743   ♦8765   ♣J8

W	N	E	S
		1♥	P
2♥	P	4♥	All Pass

Leading a spade might well blow a trick, but it's your best chance to get something going for the defense. Partner might have the ♠A or even the ♠QJ, in which case you might establish two tricks right off the bat. At duplicate, if you find partner with something in spades, just keeping declarer from making an overtrick might earn you a top score.

If you are afraid to fail, you probably will.

Chapter 18

Seeing Things—The Art of Visualization

It is accepted strategy in many endeavors to visualize. You practice seeing yourself in a foot race crossing the finish line in your goal time. You visualize a cheering audience as you finish a big speech you have been working on. You see yourself as president of the company in five years' time. In bridge, visualization is also useful, in long- and short-term exercises. You may well visualize yourself winning a major event. Along the way, you will help yourself by creating a mental picture of the opponents' hands. You will visualize a lie of the cards that will allow you to succeed—and play for it. The more you practice, the better you will get.

> ### Principle 118: Picture the other hands.

In the war that is a bridge session, you will fight up to a couple of dozen small battles, otherwise known as deals. Some will be cut and dried, but in many of them—on some nights, most of them— you will reach a critical point. At that moment, your fate will be in your own hands, and the move you make will determine whether you win or lose that small battle.

You will not always recognize the point at which you must make the critical choice, but you can train yourself to get better at recognition. In the meantime, you must practice concentration so that even if you don't recognize the critical juncture, you will at least have a chance to make the right choice.

You practice counting in part because developing that skill will help you know when the key play has arrived.

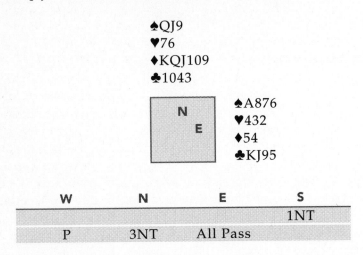

W	N	E	S
			1NT
P	3NT	All Pass	

Your partner leads the ♥Q and South wins the ace. At trick two, declarer plays a spade to dummy's queen. You win the ace. Now what?

First, review what you know about the deal so that you can begin to visualize the other two hands—and the possibilities for defeating this contract.

Between dummy and your hand, there are 17 high-card points. Declarer has shown 15–17 HCP, leaving 6 to 8 HCP for your partner. Three of his HCP are known—the ♥QJ. That means he has a king or an ace outside. It can't be just a queen because he is known to have at least 6 HCP. Could your partner have the ♠K? Perhaps he made the excellent play of ducking so that he would still have an entry after his heart suit was set up.

Another key question: Who has the ♦A?

Clearly that card is with South. If he was missing the ♦A, he would have been playing on that suit instead of spades. So South has the ♥AK and the ♦A, 11 HCP. If he is missing the ♠K, he will certainly have the ♣A, and possibly the ♣Q as well.

Partner might have ducked the ♠K, but it is more likely that South has that card. So, if South has the ♠K, you now know 14 of his HCP, and you know he cannot hold the ♣A. If he did, that would mean he had 18 HCP, too many to open 1NT.

Now you have a pretty good picture of the other two hands, so instead of woodenly returning partner's heart suit, you must try for tricks in clubs. Be sure to note the ♣10 in dummy. To make the most of your opportunity here, you must take care to play this suit properly by leading the jack, a "surrounding" play. If you play low or start with the king first, South will end up with a stopper in clubs. If you begin with the jack, South can cover with the queen, but West will then lead through dummy's ♣104 to your ♣K95. You will take four tricks and defeat the contract. You have visualized a way to defeat the contract and made the most of your opportunity, because the full deal was as follows:

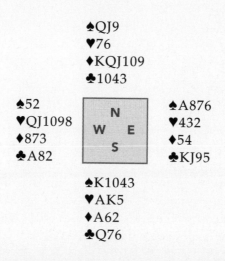

```
                    ♠QJ9
                    ♥76
                    ♦KQJ109
                    ♣1043
    ♠52                              ♠A876
    ♥QJ1098         N                ♥432
    ♦873          W   E              ♦54
    ♣A82            S                ♣KJ95
                    ♠K1043
                    ♥AK5
                    ♦A62
                    ♣Q76
```

♣ ♦ ♥ ♠

*One way to turn aspirations into reality is to visualize
where you want to go and what you want to do.*

▷ Principle 119: Don't try for the impossible.

When you find yourself at what seems to be a critical juncture and
no path seems clear, use your imagination to try to discover a way
to your goal—making your contract or defeating theirs.

You must discipline yourself to reject plays that have zero
chance of succeeding, such as a finesse for a king through an opponent who passed as dealer and who has shown up with 10 or 11
HCP. Other options may seem totally hopeless as well, but keep
looking. You know there is a better chance than zero.

On defense, when you are tempted to bang down an ace at a
critical juncture, be careful to ask yourself whether your partner
could have the king. If it's impossible given what you have discovered through the bidding and play, forget it. Your partner will lose
confidence in you if you show impatience and an unwillingness to
at least try to work out the other hands.

It's a rare deal that provides no clues whatsoever to the correct path.

♣ ♦ ♥ ♠

Patience and discipline are signs of maturity.

▷ Principle 120: Know where to look for clues.

Crafty players will try to keep their true intentions from you. It's
in their best interest not to give you clues that will help you as a
defender or as a declarer. Nevertheless, sometimes they can't help
giving away information.

In the 3NT contract earlier in this chapter, the fact that declarer
did not play on his long, strong diamond suit in dummy was an

excellent clue that he had the ace. It helped you form your picture of declarer's hand—and partner's. Remember, you're looking at your own hand and the dummy, so once you figure out one of the other hands, the fourth will come into focus as well.

Your partner's opening lead—or maybe what he *didn't* lead—will help you form a mental image of the other hands. If the opening leader against your contract seems to be going out of his way to make a passive lead, you can draw inferences—his hand is truly terrible, or he is trying to avoid giving up a trick by leading away from some dangerous holding, such as the AQ or KJ of some suit.

If an auction practically demands the lead of a suit and the opening leader chooses another, it's most likely because he has the ace of that suit. Good players rarely lead aces.

W	N	E	S
1♥	P	2♥	2♠
3♥	3♠	All Pass	

If West leads something other than a heart, there is a good chance he has the ace. That's not the only reason, of course, but experienced players usually find some other lead. While you're at it, if West does not lead a heart, you can infer with a fair degree of accuracy that he doesn't have a holding such as AK or KQ. This can provide a vital clue as you try to figure out who has what between the opponents' hands.

When an opponent has opened with a preempt at the three level or higher, but especially at the three level, and he leads his own suit against your contract, you can infer that he probably does not have a singleton. When he does lead what appears to be a singleton, you can infer that he does not have a singleton trump. This can be helpful in those situations where you are trying to decide between finessing for a queen and playing for the drop.

♣ ♦ ♥ ♠

Always keep your mind open to possibilities for improvement.

➤ Principle 121: Make assumptions when you have to.

In some settings, notably pairs, your objective will not always be clear. Because overtricks make such a difference in a pair game, your goal may be more than just making your contract or, if you are defender, defeating theirs. In the main, however, you will be trying to take enough tricks to make your contract or to defeat the one you are defending. Some contracts will have no chance of making; some will be ironclad. You can't do anything about those, but don't be too quick to put a contract into one category or the other.

Sometimes you will find yourself in a situation where there is one chance.

Suppose you are in a spade slam with ♥K6543 in dummy and ♥J105 in your hand. You have no discards in other suits and there are no trumps left in dummy. You must play this suit for one loser. What is your best chance? Can you see it? To make this contract, you must assume the player on your right has a singleton heart and that it is the ace or queen. This requires a guess, but perhaps the auction has given you some information. Perhaps your right-hand opponent opened with a preemptive bid of 3♣ or 3♦. He would be more likely in that case to have a singleton queen. In any case, you must make your assumption and play accordingly.

♣ ♦ ♥ ♠

An optimistic outlook will often give you the best chance for success.

➤ Principle 122: Be daring.

If everything in bridge were cut and dried, it would not have so many devoted followers. Players enjoy the opportunities for using their imagination and, in a highly figurative sense, swashbuckling.

There are few events more thrilling than making a creative play that works out. It's even better when such a play is made against a favored team or pair. Of course, it doesn't hurt that if you accomplish a bit of magic against an expert, he is more likely to appreciate it.

♠432   ♥AKJ872   ♦J987   ♣–

W	N	E	S
			2♥
Dbl	3♥	4♠	P
4NT	P	5♥	P
6♠	All Pass		

Do you like your chances against this slam? Do you think you will be able to cash more than one heart? Not if East-West are competent players. You don't use 4NT (Blackwood) with two quick losers in any suit. So, what do you think is your best shot?

A daring player would try the ♥2. If partner wins a surprise trick with the ♥Q—as you are fervently hoping—he won't have any trouble working out what to do next. Such an unusual lead will have suit-preference implications, so it won't take long for you to get your club ruff to defeat the slam. You are hoping the four hands are as follows:

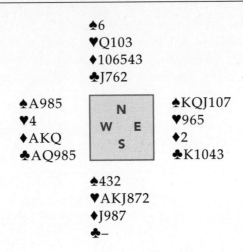

♠6
♥Q103
♦106543
♣J762

♠A985
♥4
♦AKQ
♣AQ985

♠KQJ107
♥965
♦2
♣K1043

♠432
♥AKJ872
♦J987
♣–

Your partner's raise to 3♥ on such a weak hand is relatively safe. He knows the opponents have at least a game, possibly a slam, and will be loathe to double for little reward when a bigger gain is possible. The raise does not necessarily suggest an honor in the suit, but you have little else to play for.

Underleading your hearts honors to get a club ruff is a spectacular play, but it required only that you use your imagination and be willing to take a chance. In anything but a pair game, the overtrick if your gambit didn't work would be meaningless anyway. Even in pairs, it probably wouldn't make a tremendous difference in your score.

You might be surprised what you can do if you dare to try.

Chapter 19

Working on Your Game

Once you are hooked on bridge, it will be natural for you to try to improve as rapidly as you can. Rest assured that, despite your best efforts, it will seem sometimes that you are making no progress at all. At other times, you will feel that you are seeing things more clearly than ever. That's one of the fascinations of the game. The best way to improve your game is to take up duplicate. The scoring provides a way for you to measure your progress, and you will have the opportunity to compete against some of the best players in your area. Never underestimate the value of that experience.

> **Principle 123: "Play up" as often as you can.**

In the old days, if you wanted to play in a tournament or a duplicate game, you had one choice. There was one game. If you were up to getting your brains beat in for the first few times you played, there was a wealth of experience to be had.

Nowadays, most tournaments and many clubs have games for beginners aimed at easing them into the competitive world of duplicate. This is good for those who are unsure of themselves, but the cocoon of the newcomer game can also retard your progress.

At some point, you will have to venture into the world of the "open" game, where the competition is stiffer and there are more experienced players. If you look at the open game as an opportunity rather than a death sentence, you will be well on your way to becoming one of the experts.

If you are relatively new, you don't have to "play up" every time. It's good for your ego to be a big fish in a small pond and flex your bridge muscles now and then. Don't forget, though, that unless you play up some of the time, your improvement will be much slower than you would like it to be.

♣ ♦ ♥ ♠

You must extend yourself if you are to grow as a person.

➤ Principle 124: Play with better players.

If you have a lot of money and a strong desire to improve your game in record time, you can hire a professional to play with you, just as an aspiring tennis player might take lessons from a pro.

If you don't have the funds to pay someone to play with you, there are still options. At most bridge clubs, you will find a number of good players who are willing to become mentors to up-and-coming people like you. Many clubs encourage such activity with regular "pro-am" games or special games for experts and beginners. It's one way you might meet someone who is interested in helping you— someone who remembers what it was like to struggle to improve.

It's a lot easier if you have a compatible person on the other side of the table noticing your errors and patiently explaining how you could have done better—and how you can figure it out for yourself next time.

The key to getting along with a mentor or coach is to listen to what they have to say. If you know everything already, there's little point in trying to help you.

Meeting potential mentors is another benefit of playing up, by the way. You are unlikely to meet someone who can provide substantial help if you stay in the newcomer games. If you venture into the open games, however, it will be clear you are aiming for higher achievement, and your requests for help will be met with more success.

Don't be afraid to ask for help to achieve personal growth. Someone who has undergone a similar struggle will have the experience to help you through yours.

▷ Principle 125: Read books.

There is no substitute for personal instruction. If you learned to play bridge in a class, you understand how important it is to be able to ask questions about concepts that might seem esoteric. It is also very helpful to have access to an experienced player who can answer your questions. If you are intent on learning, you will have an unlimited supply of questions.

It would be a mistake, however, for you to overlook the opportunities for learning in bridge books. You are more likely to recognize a situation if you have read about it several times in a book aimed at sharpening your dummy play.

♠QJ109
♥76
♦K102
♣AK65

```
    N

    S
```

♠AK8432
♥A4
♦AJ8
♣32

You find yourself in 6♠ and West leads a trump, to which East follows. There is a 100 percent line of play for this contract, and it's easy to spot if you have read about it enough times in your books on declarer play. If you haven't studied a lot, you might think the problem is to find the ♦Q. Nope. You win the trump lead in dummy, cash a second trump, extracting the last spade from the opponents, then you cash the top two clubs, ruff a club, re-enter dummy with a spade, and ruff the last club.

Now all you have to do is play the ♥A and your low heart. You don't care who wins the trick. If it's East, his choices will be to play a diamond, which solves that suit for you, or a heart, allowing you to discard the ♦8 from hand; then ruff in dummy. Slam made.

That's an elementary declarer play problem, and you might work it out on your own, but if you've read about it a dozen or so times before it came up at the table, you will have an excellent chance of getting it right the first time. Your partner and the opponents will look at you in a different light after that.

There are literally hundreds of books available on every subject from rudimentary declarer play to sophisticated relay bidding systems. You can avail yourself of the teachings of the greatest bridge writers who ever lived. Believe it or not, they are still in print. Many of them are still living.

Bridge literature presents a virtual smorgasbord, and if you choose wisely, you will equip yourself for rapid improvement.

♣ ♦ ♥ ♠

Experience is the best teacher, but it's not the only way you can learn.

▷ Principle 126: Practice.

There is no competitive endeavor you can think of that does not have an extended practice season. The length varies from sport to sport, but practice is essential to each. Preparation is key—and the practices invariably involve doing. Before their season begins, the Green Bay Packers actually get out on the field and tackle each other, throw footballs, and hand them off to the running backs.

Bridge is no different. You must sit at the table and hold cards in your hands to achieve the frame of mind you need to do your best. It's great—essential, even—to read about squeezes and endplays, but you must sit down against real people who are intent on beating you. That's how you get that edge, how you sharpen yourself.

The bridge club can be your best resource for practice. Few people can find a tournament every week, but most cities of any size will have at least one bridge club. There you will find the kind of competition that will keep your mind sharp.

♣ ♦ ♥ ♠

Talent without hard work equals lost opportunity.

➤ Principle 127: Watch experts.

You will learn the most by playing bridge, but there are many opportunities for players who are willing to take a break now and then and simply observe.

If you find yourself at a tournament with well-known players in attendance, consider taking a session—or even a day—off to simply watch. In bridge, a spectator is known as a kibitzer.

Even at your local club, there will be players with vast experience and expertise. You can learn a lot by simply sitting silently, perhaps taking notes. Some of what goes on may surprise you, but you will have the opportunity, perhaps between rounds, to ask about certain bids and plays you have noted. Certainly at the end of the session, it's appropriate to query the expert on why he did this or that during the session. You can be sure that he remembers everything that came up. It's highly likely he knows what all the players at the table held.

♣ ♦ ♥ ♠

Do not be too proud to ask for help.

▷ Principle 128: Ask questions.

It's happened to everyone who has played bridge for any length of time: You had a problem with a particular deal. You went down in your contract, but you had a nagging feeling that you should have made it. You feel even worse when you check the scores at the end of the game and find that you were the only declarer who managed a minus score.

That's a good time to search out one of the better players at your club and ask how he played the contract. Tell him what happened to you and see if he can shed some light on where you went wrong. It might be something very simple—a momentary blind spot that sent you off in the wrong direction. Perhaps it's a matter of technique—you simply needed a reminder of the correct way to play a certain card combination.

The better players will be able to help you sort out these enigmas. Even better, they'll ask you pertinent questions about the bidding and the defense, and you might even discover that you were "fixed" by a screwball opening lead that just happened to work out for your opponents. That will help your ego and boost your confidence.

♣ ♦ ♥ ♠

Happy people are blessed with a healthy curiosity about life and living.

▷ Principle 129: Invest the time it takes to review every game you play.

One of the principal benefits of practice is the opportunity to see where you are going wrong so that you can work on correcting the mistakes.

Football teams, for example, have coaches for linebackers, receivers, linemen, quarterbacks—you name it. There's a coach for practically every function, and they spend time during practice to reinforce what works and to change what doesn't.

That's not to say that you need one coach for finessing and another for slam bidding, but you can learn a lot from reviewing what took place in the session you just played. This is much easier at a tournament, most of which provide hand records—one of the best learning tools available—for participants.

Using the hand records, you can see every card that you and everyone else held during each deal of the session. If you grab a couple of sets on your way out the door for dinner between sessions, you and your partner can go over the bidding and play, checking to see where you could have done better. Some tough situations will come clear when you see all the hands, and you will have a better chance of remembering the right move when the situation recurs.

Do not underestimate the importance of the "work" part of teamwork.

Chapter 20

Strategies for Rubber Bridge and Teams

It's important to remember that bridge is just a game. One of the most famous bridge players of all time, Charles Goren, once said that if you can't have fun playing bridge, you should take up something else. That said, it's still a competitive endeavor, and the goal is to win. You can help yourself immensely by understanding that different forms of the game require different strategies. You will maneuver quite differently in a matchpoint pair game than you will in rubber bridge or a team game.

▷ Principle 130: Know when the contract is sacred.
If you play a variety of forms of contract bridge, you will find yourself in situations where you seriously consider risking your contract for an overtrick or two. Fortunately for you, it's easy to tell when an overtrick is important and when it's not. You are interested in overtricks pretty much only when you are playing in a pair game scored by matchpoints.

If you are playing rubber or party bridge, your objective first and foremost is to make your contract.

Consider the scoring in a team game, which is one form of duplicate. If you bid and make a vulnerable game, say 4♠, you earn your trick score of 120 plus a game bonus of 500. Therefore, taking ten tricks in this contract earns your side plus 620. If the players holding your cards at the other table also bid 4♠ but take eleven tricks, they will score 650, which in team game scoring is worth 1 International Match Point—or IMP. That's a small loss in a match with seven to nine total deals. You can easily overcome that by finding a superior contract on the next deal.

But look what happens if you go stretching for that over-trick and manage to go down for minus 100 (you're vulnerable, remember). If they score plus 620 at the other table and you are minus 100, that's a cumulative minus 720—and a loss of 12 IMPs. That's much more difficult to recover.

♣ ♦ ♥ ♠

It's not always necessary to let it all hang out to find success. A conservative approach is often best.

> **Principle 131: Know who's at the other table in an IMP game.**
In your development as a bridge player, there is no substitute for experience. It will come as no surprise, of course, that you gain experience from doing and from making mistakes.

When you were brand-new to the game, you hardly knew a finesse from a fiddle, so you couldn't be expected to know about other players and other pairs—how they play, their tendencies, their reaction to adversity.

As you gain experience, your observations will be an extra aid. You will note that some players are very aggressive, in part to make up for a conservative partner—or maybe it's just their nature. You will see that some pairs employ a bidding system that by its nature is aggressive—perhaps with super-weak 1NT openers.

When you sit down in Swiss teams or knockout teams—both played using IMPs for scoring—it will behoove you to know who is at the other table. You may not always know the other pair, but you can put the information to good use when you do.

♠K32　　　♥–　　　♦AQ72　　♣KQ10987

W	N	E	S
	1NT	P	?

Unless you have very sophisticated methods, you have a problem. You know you're in the slam zone, but it does you no good to ask for aces (in most systems, that would be accomplished with a bid of 4♣, a convention known as Gerber). If your partner shows only one ace, you could still be on for a slam in clubs. Your partner could have any of a number of hands that would make a club slam a pianola (vernacular for a hand that is so easy it plays itself) or at least a favorite to make.

The trouble is there is no way to be 100 percent sure that your hand will fit with your partner's. One way to decide whether to shoot it out and just blast into 6♣ is to consider who will be holding these cards at the other table. Do you know the pair to be very aggressive? If so, it's likely they will land in 6♣. If you assume they will be in slam, here is what you will consider: If we both bid 6♣ and it makes, we're even. If we both bid it and it goes down, we're even. If they bid it and we don't and it makes, we lose 13 IMPs. If we don't bid it, we're betting that the slam goes down because we are almost certain they will be in slam at the other table. That's a pretty good hand to hold opposite a strong 1NT opener. Betting that it won't make slam probably will not be a winner in the long run. Even when it's supposed to go down, the opponents may slip up and let you make it. They might try to cash the ♥A (your void) and find dummy with ♥KQJx in that suit. That's three discards after you ruff.

It's a different proposition if the pair at the other table is known to be conservative. It's still tempting to sail into slam even if you know the other pair won't be there. You will have to judge the state of your match to determine whether you are willing to risk a big swing. If you believe you have a comfortable lead, it's probably best to be conservative.

♣ ♦ ♥ ♠

Do not underestimate the value of knowing the opposition.

▷ Principle 132: Understand the influence of vulnerability.

You must be careful when you are vulnerable, especially with your overcalls. This is especially true in rubber bridge or in team events. If you go for a big number in a pairs game, it's just one deal, a small fraction of your total score. If you go for a big number in rubber bridge, it will mean money out of your pocket—and your partner's pocket. In a team game, you have three other people to worry about—your partner and your teammates at the other table.

Big penalties are not the only way that vulnerability affects your actions, however. In a team game, vulnerability can have a profound effect on your attitude about bidding game. A look at the scoring makes it easy to figure out why you should be more aggressive when you are vulnerable—where game bidding is concerned, that is.

♠84   ♥KQ1098   ♦AJ54   ♣A5

W	N	E	S
			1♥
P	2♥	P	?

Holding this hand as South in a pairs game, you probably would simply pass, content to take your plus score. If the opponents balance, you will compete to 3♥. If your partner puts down a hand that allows you to take ten tricks, you won't be too concerned. Hardly anyone will bid the game, so you will be average or very close to it. If you make a move and end up with a minus score, it will be close to a zero. The odds are in favor of your passing.

In a team game, it's all different. You care only about beating the pair at the other table, so your thinking changes.

Say you stop in 2♥ and make ten tricks. That's plus 170. If you are not vulnerable, the score for bidding and making 4♥ would be 420. The difference of 250 translates to 6 IMPs. If you bid game and go down and they stop in 2♥ at the other table, you lose 50 versus 140, which translates to 5 IMPs. You risk losing 5 IMPs for a possible gain of 6 IMPs. It's about a wash.

When you are vulnerable, however, the reward is much greater. The score for 4♥ bid and made is 620. Subtract 170 and the difference—450—translates to 10 IMPs. If you bid game and go down, that's minus 100 versus 140, which is a 6-IMP difference. So you are risking a 6-IMP loss, but the potential gain is 10 IMPs. The odds are much better. That's why you push a little more when you are vulnerable.

♣ ♦ ♥ ♠

If you never take a risk, you will not know what it is to live.

▷ Principle 133: Be cautious with your penalty doubles.

In team games, you will be aggressive in bidding game, but you will be conservative in wielding the proverbial ax—the penalty double. You will almost never double a part score higher than 2♦ without a trump stack.

The reason is simple. If you double an opponent in 2♥ and he makes it, that's game. In other words, by doubling you have put your opponent in game—at the two level. Note that doubling 1NT, 2♣, or 2♦ does not produce a game bonus. Whereas 2♥ doubled is 470 or 670 depending on vulnerability; 1NT, 2♣, or 2♦ doubled is only 180 if it makes.

Even if they're already in game, be careful about doubling based solely on a trump stack. The warning provided by the double might be just what declarer needs to make the contract. You could turn plus 50 or 100 into minus 590 or 790.

Another caution: Even if you are sure that the contract you are doubling is going down, be sure before you pull out that red X from the bid box that they don't have another contract to run to. This is not meant to make you timid about doubling—when they're way overboard, don't hesitate to collect your due for the undertricks. Those are valuable points in a team game.

♣ ♦ ♥ ♠

It's okay to go out on a limb. Just be sure it will support your weight.

▶ Principle 134: Don't be a "steamer."

It's important to keep emotion out of your bridge game. You will face plenty of obstacles to success—combative opponents, unexpected distributions, bad luck—without making an adversary of yourself. That's just what you will be if you do not maintain a cool, calm demeanor. Do not get into the habit of "steaming."

A steamer is a player who, after going down 1100 because of a poorly judged overcall, bids game with almost no play on the next board—or makes an insane penalty double to try to prove something to the opponents.

Such decisions are made on emotion, not logic, and if you cannot play a logical bridge game, you will be a loser in the long run.

Consider how much thinking you must do in a typical bridge game. You must count cards and high-card points, gather information from the bidding and play, process it, and draw reasonable conclusions. How can you do all of this if your mind is cluttered with emotion? The answer is you can't.

Steaming is losing bridge. Get that straight and you're on your way to success.

♣ ♦ ♥ ♠

*The only thing you prove by letting anger and
frustration guide you is that you lack maturity.*

➤ Principle 135: Maintain a healthy optimism.

You've heard the classic question about whether you're the one who sees a glass as half empty or half full. It's a cliché, to be sure, but a common trait among winning bridge players is a uniformly optimistic outlook.

There is a fine line, of course, between optimism and impulsively rash behavior, but you have to believe you will succeed. You don't wait to bid a slam until you are 100 percent sure it will make. Just because you are playing a team with lots more experience, you don't concede defeat before the match starts. If you believe the cards will fall your way and that you will make the right decisions, you have more than a fighting chance.

Your outlook on life, if positive and upbeat,
will profoundly influence your mental and physical health.

Chapter 21

Strategies for Pairs

If you take up duplicate, which is highly recommended, most of the games you play will be pairs games, scored by matchpoints. As you gain experience, you will find yourself taking positions and actions that you would not consider in a team game. Some of the differences are clear—you will make close doubles of part scores that would be unthinkable in a team game, and you will risk your contract for overtricks on occasion. You will find that luck is much more prevalent in pairs than you might think. A pair game is still bridge, but it will behoove you to understand how it differs from other forms of the game.

> ➤ **Principle 136: Know how to handle part scores, games, and slams.**
Sometimes the cards run one way or the other—North-South have most of the high cards one night; East-West dominate the next. In the main, however, it's more or less an even split, and in a pair game you will find yourself in a fight for the part score more often than not.

You will find that a card full of plus scores will be a winning card most of the time. Remember, the form of scoring puts a premium on outscoring the other players sitting in your direction. That may mean your objective is to end up with a smaller minus than the other pairs sitting your way, but you must always keep in mind that your true opponents are the pairs sitting in your direction.

In general, if game is out of the question, you will try for the best-scoring part score. Here, 1NT or 2NT lead the way—making eight tricks in 1NT is good for plus 120, whereas eight tricks in hearts or spades score plus 110. In diamonds or clubs, eight tricks will get you plus 90. That doesn't mean you try to bid no-trump on every deal—sometimes the ruffing value of playing in a suit contract will produce more tricks than no-trump. Plus 130 for 3♦ making four will always beat 2NT making two (plus 120).

Never lose sight of the fact that you don't have to outscore the other pairs by hundreds of points. Any margin is good enough.

In most clubs, you will find that the pairs are pretty aggressive, so you should not make major adjustments regarding game bidding. Slams are another matter, however. If you bid a slam in a typical matchpoint game and go down, you have booked yourself for a zero or near-zero. The odds of taking twelve tricks must be well above 50 percent. As for grand slams, you better be able to count thirteen tricks. Going down in a grand slam in a pair game is death—and you will be annoyed to find that some of the pairs won't even be in a *small* slam.

♣ ♦ ♥ ♠

Always be mindful of your objective, and ready to change it when necessary.

▷ Principle 137: Learn to be aggressive.
Matchpoints is not a game for the timid. You must be ready to mix it up to have any hope of success in a pair game. You will find that the opponents are in your auctions as often as they can possibly be, and you must pay them back in kind.

♠5   ♥1043   ♦KQJ1076   ♣K54

W	N	E	S
1♥	P	2NT	?

East's 2NT bid is conventional, indicating a game-forcing raise in hearts. Now is not the time for you to consider that you have "only" 9 high-card points. You have a good suit. Speak up. Yes, you could be doubled and go down a bunch, but using that as an excuse for passing is losing bridge. There are more good things that could happen if you bid. You might find that your partner has a good fit with you in diamonds and you might engineer a successful "sacrifice" against their certain game contract. Don't worry that your partner will think you have a great hand. How could you, with West opening the bidding and East professing to have enough for game? It's also possible that bidding 3♦ will throw a monkey wrench into their bidding and make it difficult for them to find the top spot. This hand actually came up in a tournament, and the bid of 3♦ completely derailed East-West, who stopped in 6♥ when 7♥ was trivial.

That's just one way of being aggressive. In a pair game, you will go out of your way to "balance" when the opponents have settled into a comfortable part score. Your objective will be to push them up a level, perhaps so high that they go down. You love those plus scores!

♠Q8765	♥8	♦Q103	♣A943

W	N	E	S
		1♥	P
2♥	P	P	?

This is a clear-cut bid of 2♠. The fact that East-West have stopped in 2♥ indicates that your partner has some high cards. In the balancing seat, you are bidding the values you expect your partner to have. Of course, he might also have a singleton spade and some good holding in hearts, in which case you might be doubled and go down much more than East-West were going to get in 2♥. If you pass, you are playing scared, a sure way to lose.

The brass ring will not jump into your hands. You much reach for it.

➤ Principle 138: Balance your way to success—or not.

One of the principal lessons you will learn with experience in pairs is that you must not let the opposition go easily. Some partnerships have been known to make a pact that they will never let the opponents play undoubled lower than 2NT. In other words, if the opponents stop between 1♣ and 2♠, someone is going to push them higher or double, even at the risk of being doubled themselves.

Obviously, this is silly. There will be many occasions when you refrain from doubling or otherwise balancing because you know the opponents are in the wrong contract. Far be it from you to disturb a contract that you know is wrong.

♠J108   ♥Q4   ♦K43   ♣QJ1093

W	N	E	S
1♣	P	P	?

If you pass, West will be playing 1♣, which seems to fly in the face of the dictum about pushing the opponents whenever you can. Think about it, though. Your partner is bound to be short in clubs, yet he took no action, which is indicative of a weak hand. East has already announced a bust, so West must have a very strong hand. If you take some action, it's possible East-West will find a fit in a major suit, which will improve their contract immeasurably. West might have enough high-card strength to make 1♣, but he probably won't make much more than that with your stack in clubs. Be happy with what the Fates has provided. Pass.

Balancing always carries risk. One of them is what is known as "balancing them into game." It's very annoying—especially to your partner—to hear an auction such as the following.

W	N	E	S
1♠	P	P	2♣
4♠	All Pass		

When this contract is made, you feel like a fool. There they were, languishing in 1♠ when opener had enough to bid and make game opposite a partner who couldn't keep the bidding open.

If you want to do your own scientific analysis, purchase a software program for your computer that deals random hands with certain patterns. Evaluate for yourself what percentage of the hands work out better to pass.

Do not stubbornly cling to strategies proven not to work.
If it fails ten times in a row, it's not likely to work the eleventh time either.

▷ Principle 139: Know when to double.
It pays to be aggressive in pairs, and if you follow that philosophy you will often be within an inch of disaster. Since the difference between a top and a zero can be one little trick, you will be in there fighting for every advantage, no matter how small it seems. In the course of this combat, you will be on the edge frequently, and you should remember that any opponents with a semblance of competence will also be there.

To be a winner, you must be willing to double them into game now and then to protect your turf.

It's most tempting to double when the opponents are vulnerable. A one-trick set will be enough to earn you a fine score. Everyone knows the risks are much greater in a vulnerable state, but that should not influence you to the point of never taking anything even resembling aggressive action when you are "red."

You can't make an omelet without breaking some eggs.

> **Principle 140: Know when it's right to risk your contract.**

The safety play usually involves giving up a trick you could probably win to be sure your primary objective—making the contract—is fulfilled. The safety play is a valuable tool in rubber bridge or teams. At matchpoints, safety plays are mostly reserved for unusually good (or doubled) contracts. Too often, the matchpoint price you pay for assuring your contract via a safety play is too high.

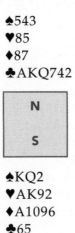

♠543
♥85
♦87
♣AKQ742

N
S

♠KQ2
♥AK92
♦A1096
♣65

West leads the ♠J against your 3NT. East takes the ace and returns a spade. You win and assess your contract. You have eight top tricks, with lots of possibilities in clubs. The opponents have five clubs between them, and if the clubs split 3-2, you have eleven tricks, and you might even end up with twelve if the opponents discard poorly or (very rarely) a red-suit squeeze operates on East.

Five missing cards in a suit will divide 3-2 67.83 percent of the time, but 28.26 percent of the time, they will go 4-1 (you don't consider a 5-0 split because you can't do anything about that). So, more than a quarter of the time you will find a 4-1 split. How do you deal with it? Well, you play a low club from hand and a low club from dummy. You set up the suit while you still have a way to get to dummy's good club tricks.

If you play the top three clubs and find the suit divided 4-1, you can set up the suit by playing a fourth round, but there's no way to get back to dummy to take the two good clubs.

This is a no-brainer at teams, but it's different at matchpoints. Since the clubs will go 3-2 more than two-thirds of the time, if you duck a club to assure your contract, two-thirds of the time you will take ten tricks while most everyone else will be taking eleven. That will give you a zero or very close to it. When the suit does divide 4-1, you will get a top, but only on 28 percent of the occasions.

Of course, if you judge that you are in a contract few players are likely to reach (usually game or slam), it can pay off handsomely to assure your contract against bad breaks. Also, if you are doubled and a safety play will see you home, have no compunction about taking it.

♣ ♦ ♥ ♠

When you're thinking about taking a chance,
consider whether the reward is worth the risk.

> **Principle 141: Know when to "play down the middle."**

If you play long enough, some day your partner will move up close to you late in a pair game and say something along these lines:

"Partner, if we just sit in our chairs for the next three rounds, we will win this thing."

What your partner is trying to tell you is that his estimate of your game is that it's going so well that there's no need to take risks from here on out. No close doubles, no aggressive slams, no unusual preempts looking to create swings. Average scores will be enough. He could be wrong, of course, but experienced players usually know when they have a big game going.

That doesn't mean you forget your normal aggressive style. You still balance, you still overcall four-card suits when you have the right hand for it, you still open 3♣ with a seven-card suit and little else. Pulling back too much can result in just as many zeroes as going nuts.

But your aggression is controlled and you don't go out of your way looking for swings.

If things are going your way, sit back and enjoy it. Don't try to create what's not there. Don't be greedy for a 75 percent game when you've got 70 percent in the bag.

When fortune smiles on you, enjoy it. Hard luck may be right around the corner.

Chapter 22

Tricks of the Trade

You know Stayman, Blackwood, negative doubles, and Jacoby Transfers. You may have learned all of these in bridge class—or from a book. Unfortunately, everything you need to know is not necessarily widely available. That's why it's a good idea to check out a few less-than-well-known ideas.

> **Principle 142: Learn when to get in against their 1NT opener.**

Anyone who has played bridge a long time can recall the days when, if you opened 1NT (16–18 high-card points in the old days), you got a free run in the auction. Who would dare to interfere when opener was so strong?

That kind of attitude was debunked a long time ago. Today, all manner of systems exist with the express purpose of making it easier to get into the auction after a 1NT opener. None of them is perfect, but it's accepted that anything is better than nothing—nothing being a "natural" system (whatever you bid is what you have). It's also accepted that it's a good idea to bid if you can.

It's not within the scope of this book to cover the various systems for getting in when they open 1NT, but there are guidelines for determining when you should—and should not—enter the auction.

First, forget about doubling when you have a balanced hand with a strong 1NT opener yourself. It is extremely difficult to defeat

1NT when you continually have to lead from your strength into opener's strength. You are, in essence, endplayed at trick one, and an astute declare will keep throwing you back in to his advantage.

You should, therefore, reserve your doubles for hands with long suits and entries.

When you have a two-suited hand, there is a simple guideline for determining whether you should enter the auction. First, understand about losers. Each suit has a potential three losers: Count a loser for every missing ace, king, or queen, assuming three cards or more. A doubleton counts as two losers, a singleton one, and a void no losers.

♠54　　♥AQ54　　♦KJ94　　♣QJ7

This hand has two losers in spades, one in hearts, two in diamonds, and two in clubs, for a total of seven.

Now, to determine whether you should enter the auction with your two-suited bid, take the number of losers in your whole hand and subtract it from the number of cards in your two longest suits. If the sum is one or zero, pass. If the number is two or higher, get in there with whatever system you like to play. The more shape you have, the better are your prospects.

♠A7654　　♥K109876　　♦4　　♣7

Only 7 HCP, but the 6-5 shape is great for competing—and the formula is right. You have two losers in spades, two in hearts, and one each in diamonds and clubs for a total of six. You have eleven cards in your two long suits, so bid 'em up.

♣ ♦ ♥ ♠

It's the worst kind of thinking to adhere to a policy simply because "that's the way we've always done it." Change is often invigorating.

▷ Principle 143: Take advantage of Trash Stayman.

You were taught that it takes 8 high-card points to bid Stayman. That's meant to assure that if you ended up stopping in 2NT, sometimes a very precarious spot, you will have adequate resources.

There is one time when you can correctly bid Stayman with *zero* high-card points. It happens when you are very weak and have one particular feature to your hand: club shortness.

♠9876   ♥6532   ♦10654   ♣7

This is an extreme example, but the point is that if your partner opens 1NT, you should bid Stayman (2♣) with this hand, planning to pass whatever your partner says in reply. Of course, you know the one suit your partner will not mention is clubs. When you bid Stayman, partner is required to bid a major if he has one and to bid 2♦ if he doesn't. He will never bid clubs—it's not part of the system. You can, therefore, pass and let your partner take advantage of the power of trumps, whatever that might end up being.

It's true that if your partner bids 2♦ that he might have only two of them, but you're willing to take that chance because you know for a certainty that he is not going to enjoy playing 1NT with your hand as the dummy. It will be a slaughter. Give your partner a break. Bid Stayman. As long as you are very short in clubs, you don't even have to have four of each of the other suits.

♣ ♦ ♥ ♠

Give yourself the freedom to be creative.

▷ Principle 144: Include Exclusion Blackwood.

You are often warned against bidding 4NT to ask for aces when you are void in a suit because in more cases than not you will not know what to do once you receive partner's answer. If you are missing one ace, you could be on for a grand slam if the missing ace is in your void suit. But if the missing ace is in a different suit—well, you get the picture.

The solution to that dilemma—and a pathway to more accurate bidding—is to employ what is known as Exclusion Blackwood. Nowadays, it is described more often as Exclusion Key Card Blackwood because the king of the agreed trump suit has become one of the key cards that is enumerated in the answer to 4NT.

Regardless of whether you are interested simply in aces or in key cards, there is a way of asking about them that provides for an answer you can use. Whenever the trump suit is agreed, an unusual jump in a suit is designated as an ace- or key card-asking bid excluding the suit in which you jump.

W	N	E	S
			1♠
P	2NT	P	5♣

This unusual jump after partner has made a game-forcing raise of your spade suit has no logical meaning. Once you find one fit, you normally do not go looking for another. If you were making a cuebid (showing a control), there would be no need to jump. The bid of 5♣ says to partner, "Tell me about the number of aces (or key cards) in your hand outside of the club suit." You might have a hand such as the following.

♠AKQ106   ♥KQJ109   ♦A43   ♣–

If you simply jump to 4NT, asking for aces, and your partner admits to having one ace, you won't know whether to bid a small slam or a grand slam in your suit. If partner has the ♥A, seven should be trivial. If it's the ♣A, however, you can be certain you aren't making a grand slam. If you are using Exclusion Blackwood, you will know.

If you and your partner decide to employ this convention, be prepared to screw it up the first couple of times it comes up. No one ever misunderstands 4NT, but somehow the meaning of a jump in a suit can escape you until you get used to it.

This is a convention well worth studying and including in your repertoire of bidding agreements. It doesn't come up often, but when it does, it's worth its weight in gold.

♣ ♦ ♥ ♠

Never underestimate the power of information.

▶ Principle 145: Learn useful "rules."

You know about the Rule of 11 (for spot card leads), 15 (how to decide whether to open in fourth seat), and the Rule of 8 (a helpful guide in competitive auctions). They can be useful if viewed in context and applied properly.

There's another "rule" that can be of great assistance—the Rule of 7.

Here's how it works. If you are declarer in a no-trump contract, holding the ace in the suit the opponents have led, you might wonder sometimes how many times you should hold up. You have been taught, of course, that it is often effective to hold up an ace so that when you have to let the opponents in, the one who gets in might be out of that suit and unable to return it. This is an especially valuable strategy when you will have to take a finesse that could lose to the partner of the opening leader. You want that person to be out of his partner's suit—or at least for the suit to divide in such a way that they can't defeat you.

♠865
♥AQJ43
♦A6
♣1098

♠A43
♥109
♦KQ7
♣A7654

West leads the ♠K against your contract of 3NT. How many times should you hold up?

Here's how the Rule of 7 works. Take the number of cards you hold in your hand and dummy, subtract from seven. The answer will be the number of times you should hold up your ♠A. In this case, it would be once. If you duck once and West continues the suit, you win and take the heart finesse, which you must do to make your contract. If East has another spade, that means the suit has broken 4-3 and the defenders can take no more than three spades and the ♥K. If dummy had one fewer spade and one more diamond, say, your calculation would have resulted in a sum of two, meaning you would need to duck twice. There will be times, of course, when you will want to win the first trick because you fear a switch to another suit. That's where judgment comes in. Rules of this type are there to help you and are not inviolable.

You don't always have to take advice from those with more experience than you, but it cannot hurt to listen.

▷ Principle 146: An oddly even proposition.

You will face many situations where it is necessary to calculate the odds of two different lines of play so as to select one. Few players can recall all the mathematical tables and sets of percentages. There is plenty to think about without cluttering up your mind. A basic knowledge can be very useful, however, and should be part of your repertoire.

Here's a tidbit many players do not know: When there are an odd number of cards outstanding in a suit, they tend to divide more evenly than when there are an even number of cards. In other words, when there are five cards missing, they are more likely to divide 3-2 (67.83 percent) than 4-1 (28.26 percent). When there are six cards missing, however, they are more likely to divide 4-2 (46.88 percent) than 3-3 (31.75 percent). The same goes for three and four. Three cards divide 2-1, 78 percent of the time and 3-0, 22 percent. Four cards split 3-1, 49.74 percent, 2-2 only 40.7 percent.

Information of this kind can be useful when varying lines of play depend on suit distributions. If you have a choice between trying for a 3-3 split or taking a finesse, understand that the 3-3 break is less than 32 percent, whereas a finesse is usually a 50 percent proposition.

♠AK654
♥83
♦AQ62
♣K4

♠72
♥AKQJ72
♦53
♣Q86

W	N	E	S
	1♠	P	2♥
P	2NT	P	4♥
P	6♥	All Pass	

West leads the ♣A and switches to the ♦10. Your partner's bidding is optimistic, to be kind, but his excitability is not germane at this moment. What you must concentrate on is taking twelve tricks. What is your thinking?

If you are playing against good players, you should be aware that West knows you would prefer to try more than one line of play to make your contract. For example, if West woodenly continues with a club, you win in dummy, pull trumps, and play the top two spades, ruffing the third round. If the suit proves to be 3-3, both dummy's remaining spades will be good and you can claim, discarding your losing diamond on one of them. If the spades prove to be 4-2, you will have to rely on the diamond finesse for your twelfth trick. By switching to the diamond at trick two, West is making you decide immediately what to do.

In the end, you may decide to go with the odds and take the 50 percent diamond finesse rather than relying on the 31.75 percent chance that spades are 3-3.

The factor you must consider is West's level of experience and expertise. If West is a newer player, he is unlikely to be leading from a king against a slam. You will be better off, in that case, to rise with the ♦A and hope for a 3-3 spade split. If your inexperienced opponent in the West seat has led from the ♦K at trick two (and spades break 4-2 or worse), be sure to compliment him on his tough defense.

The more you know about the potential risks of a given situation, the better prepared you will be to make a decision.

> **Principle 147: Give suit preference at trick one in obvious situations.**

One of the keys to success at bridge is taking care of your partner—not making bids that your partner won't understand or esoteric plays your partner is unlikely to work out. If you protect your partner, if you keep him from making errors when it's within your power to do so, he will reciprocate. You will be a smoothly working team.

There is a situation that is more common than you might think—the opportunity to give your partner a suit-preference signal at trick one. It occurs when you know your partner is leading a singleton. It may seem strange to say that you will know, but it's true. The auction, the cards in your hand, the dummy—all of them will tell you that your partner is hoping to get a ruff later in the play.

If you and your partner are on the same wavelength, you can help him find your entry so he can get that ruff—assuming, of course, that you have an entry.

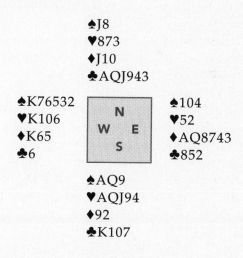

```
                        ♠J8
                        ♥873
                        ♦J10
                        ♣AQJ943

    ♠K76532         ┌─────────┐      ♠104
    ♥K106           │    N    │      ♥52
    ♦K65            │  W   E  │      ♦AQ8743
    ♣6             │    S    │      ♣852
                    └─────────┘
                        ♠AQ9
                        ♥AQJ94
                        ♦92
                        ♣K107
```

W	N	E	S
			1♥
P	2♣	P	3♣
P	3♥	P	4♥
All Pass			

You are East. West starts with the ♣6. If you can't tell that's a singleton, you must have been asleep during the auction. Note that dummy has six clubs and South raised the suit. You have three of them. West's ♣6 is the singleton-est card, to coin a phrase, you're ever going to see. Furthermore, everyone knows it's a stiff, another name for a singleton. You, declarer, dummy, all the kibitzers, maybe even the ten o'clock news—you all know it's West's only club.

So what do you do about it?

You can infer that West is confident he will get in before trumps are drawn, so he probably has the ♥A or the ♥K with at least two others. He's hoping to get you in for a ruff. It's your job to tell him how to do it.

This is something you and your partner should talk over. When one of you leads an obvious singleton, it's the partner's job to indicate where a potential entry might be. You do that by carefully selecting the card that you play to the first trick.

You have the ♣852. It can't possibly matter which one you play in terms of trick taking—you aren't taking any tricks in this suit. You can therefore use your cards to signal to partner where you have an entry. In this case, it's the ♦A, so you would play the ♣2 at trick one, a suit-preference signal indicating the lower of the two other suits. If you had the ♠A instead of the ♦A, you would play the ♣8, also a suit-preference signal indicating the higher of the two other suits.

So declarer, knowing West has led a singleton, will win the trick in dummy and play a heart to the ace, followed by the ♥Q, hoping that West had only two hearts. West will foil the plan, however. After winning the ♥K, he will play a diamond to your ace, take his ruff and cash the ♦K for the setting trick.

If you weren't using this signal, your partner would have to guess which suit to return, and if he guessed wrong, declarer would make his contract with an overtrick.

♣ ♦ ♥ ♠

There are few things more satisfying than accomplishing a goal through teamwork.

➤ Principle 148: Write it down.

Some players, particularly those with several regular partners, have trouble remembering their bidding systems or all of the features of various conventions, some of which can be complex.

It's gratifying to construct a bidding system you are comfortable with and can show off to others, but it can be frustrating to have difficulty remembering everything you agree to play.

It can help you a lot if you write your bidding system out by hand. It may seem surprising, but this will engrave it in your mind much more readily than if you simply read a written page. To do the writing, you must concentrate on what you are doing, and when you are finished you will be able to recall as in a photograph what you wrote. It will come to mind that much easier.

If you have multiple partners, try this trick: Get to the game ten minutes early and, using an already-filled-out convention card for your partner of the day, do another one from top to bottom. You will be much less likely to forget what you are playing with this particular partner if you have just filled in the convention card blanks yourself.

♣ ♦ ♥ ♠

Sometimes the simplest solutions are the best.

Chapter 23

Gaining a True Understanding of Bridge

Forget about ever mastering the game of bridge. The best players in the world will tell you they can't do it. That's not to say that they don't enjoy it—or that you can't have fun playing bridge without becoming a world champion. It's an enormously frustrating game, but it is also full of rewards and thrills. You don't have to play at an elevated level to love bridge, but you have to understand that it will make you tear your hair sometimes.

▷ Principle 149: Be prepared to be humbled.

Bridge has a way of bringing you down to earth in ways you don't expect and at moments when you are least prepared.

You might have just played against two professionals in a tournament and made a doubled contract for a complete top score. Then you sit down at the table against an elderly couple who look like they wouldn't harm a fly—and they kill you.

Last week you were on the winning team in a big tournament out of town. This week, you and your partner have to stage a major rally on the last round of the club game to get to 45 percent.

What's going on?

It's the bridge gods, making sure you don't take the game for granted. Enjoy the thrill of victory, but know that you will also become well acquainted with the agony of defeat. That's just the way bridge is.

Take life as it comes. Don't get too high from your triumphs or too low from your defeats.

> ### Principle 150: Learn to laugh at disaster.

This happened at a club game in early 2004. Declarer was in a normal 4♥ contract.

♠65
♥QJ87
♦K5
♣KQ543

N
S

♠AQ8
♥A10965
♦A7
♣J109

The opening lead of a low diamond was made and declarer (South) played the king from dummy, following after a brief pause—with the ace! She had just compressed two diamond tricks into one and fashioned a loser in a suit where there had been none. Declarer's partner, the dummy, looked on with incredulity. The opponents were bemused.

When the contract had been played out—declarer made ten tricks for plus 420 and a very poor score—what do you think the two players did? They did exactly what you're supposed to do when you do something silly like that, even when it turns into disaster—they had a good laugh about it. After the game, they laughed about it some more.

This is the kind of silly thing than can happen to anyone—getting a trick ahead of yourself and having what might euphemistically be called a brain cramp. Some people like to say, when asked why they did something so silly, "A cow flew by."

If you can bring yourself to laugh at these mini-tragedies, you will be on your way to being a winner.

♣ ♦ ♥ ♠

You can't turn back time to undo your mistakes.
Try to learn from them for the future.

▷ Principle 151: Understand that bridge can be a cruel game.

This will happen to you one day. You will conduct what feels like the world's greatest auction to a marvelous grand slam, with AKQ765 opposite 432 in your trump suit—and one of your grinning opponents will be holding J1098. The odds of this happening are less than one in ten, but it will happen.

Bridge comes with no guarantees. Your best-laid plans will sometimes blow up in your face. Sometimes it will be your error, sometimes your partner will seem to be conspiring with the opponents, but just as often it will be fate.

One of the most famous bridge hands of all time was played by Eddie Kantar, a great player and one of the best bridge writers the world has ever known. He was playing in the Bermuda Bowl, the premier event in all of bridge, against an Italian team that seemed like they just couldn't lose to their American rivals.

At one point in a very close match for the championship, Kantar heard his Italian opponent on the right bidding clubs and bidding them again. The auction seemed to go on forever, but Kantar had a secret. He was looking at the ♣K10, and he was behind the guy who was bidding clubs like he had a million of them. Kantar was certain his king was going to take a trick.

Eventually, the Italians reached 7♣, and Kantar was silently laughing up his sleeve—at last, the Italians would get their come-uppance, bidding too high and going down. Clearly they had had a misunderstanding if they had settled in a grand slam missing the king of trumps (it just isn't done in expert circles). Even better, he had the trump king where it was going to take a trick, which was all they needed to defeat the contract.

Imagine Kantar's shock and chagrin when, after he made his opening lead, dummy hit with—gasp!—the ♣AQ! The terrible grand slam was bid and made. The Americans, particularly Kantar, felt as though someone had kicked them in the stomach.

It will help you through these episodes if you can remember a very important fact: You have probably benefited from twists of fate that were visited upon others. In fact, if you have played long enough, that's almost certainly true.

♣ ◆ ♥ ♠

There are no guarantees that life will be fair. Be prepared for bumps in the road.

▷ Principle 152: Learn to cope with losing streaks.

No one can win every time, particularly in a pair game, which can have an exceedingly random flavor to it. Some pairs will do better than others, and some will achieve enviably consistent results, but no one will take home the top prize every time. This is particularly true in expert circles, where the standard of play is very high and there are many players worthy of victory.

Even with this knowledge, it's tough when you hit the inevi-table streak where it seems that nothing goes right for you.

Many factors can bring on what seems like a losing streak. If you have started a new partnership, it will take some time for the two of you to mesh. In that period, you will have many "accidents" or situations that require some fine-tuning. If you are compatible in terms of temperament and goals, hang in there. It will be worth it.

Another contributor to a lackluster run can be a plateau of sorts. Your development as a player will not have a straight line up. You may progress rapidly at first, but most players hit a level and stay there a while before starting to move again. This can feel like a losing streak.

Then there will be the good, old-fashioned strings of bad luck, compounded by poor play and topped off with a feeling of frustration that becomes a distraction.

Expect a losing streak. Treat your development as a player like a marathon. It's a long way from start to finish, and if you maintain a steady pace, refuse to get down on yourself and keep trying, you will make it to the finish with valuable experience.

♣ ♦ ♥ ♠

You will be sorely disappointed if you expect perfection on the very first try.

▷ Principle 153: Learn to handle frustration.

In many ways, bridge is a strange game. As you know, it's not that difficult to learn the rules—tricks, bidding, suits, trumps, etc. The mechanics of the game are not what you would call challenging.

Serious students of the game will find, however, that true learning can be a slow process. Just when you think you have mastered a particular area, you find out that you haven't really scratched the surface.

If you try to commit the game to "rules," you will find that for every one you learn, there are a dozen exceptions. The real learning comes in trying to figure out when the normal or expected bid or play won't work. Of course, even after you have reached that stage, you face the challenge of working out what among the alternative choices *will* work.

It can all be pretty frustrating. Compounding your exasperation will be your own problem areas. Most players new to the game consider defense to be the most difficult area. For many others, learning to count is very difficult because it seems so overwhelming a task at first.

There is a lot to assimilate if you want to do more than throw cards on the table.

The great thing about the learning process in bridge is that as you gain experience you realize how much of a challenge it is to get where you want to go. When you take a step forward, even a small one, you realize the significance and gain a lot of satisfaction from that.

♣ ♦ ♥ ♠

If you maintain focus on your objective, the difficulties you encounter on the way to success will not seem so momentous.

▷ Principle 154: Understand luck.

When you first hear about duplicate bridge—where everyone plays the same hands again and again during a session and scoring is done by comparisons—you think: Finally, someone has taken luck out of the game.

Not so.

It's true, duplicate represents a stark contrast to rubber or party bridge because in that form of the game the hands are played, then the cards are mixed together and dealt again. If the cards are running your way, you win. If not, you lose.

In duplicate, you can win with bad cards. If you are sitting East-West and the cards are running North-South—not an uncommon occurrence—most East-West pairs will be writing minuses into the scorecards. The winners will be the East-West pair with smaller minuses that the others.

Where luck figures in has nothing to do with whether cards are running one way or the other—mostly the high-card strength is evenly distributed. The luck factor has a lot to do with being in the right place at the right time—or vice versa.

It's great luck if you are sitting at the table when an opponent has a brain cramp and passes a cuebid. They're at the five level in a 3-1 fit. You just got a top from being in the right place at the right time.

It's awful luck if you're sitting at the table against a pair of experts when the only way to make a contract is via a complex squeeze or endplay. You can be sure most of the other players won't make the contract, so when the expert brings the contract home against you, Lady Luck has just kicked you in the shorts. Or suppose your opponents foul up their auction and stop in 2NT with 27 high-card points between them—but no more than eight tricks can be made because of bad breaks in key suits. Screwed again.

Luck is a huge part of the game, especially in duplicate. You can create your own luck by being aggressive in the bidding, giving the opponents more opportunities to make mistakes. You will be viewed as a "lucky" player if you learn and apply good card play technique. You will be "luckier" if you take well-reasoned chances as declarer and as a defender.

Count yourself blessed—and act accordingly—
if opportunity knocks a second time.

Chapter 24

Developing Your Style

Bridge is a game that welcomes everyone: professionals such as attorneys and physicians, people as diverse as athletes and blue-collar workers, college students, and grandmothers. The people who love bridge run the gamut. At a bridge club, you might see an eleven-year-old boy playing with a ninety-year-old woman. The toughest player in your club might be 5-foot-2 and weigh 110 pounds. Appearances notwithstanding, every bridge player has a style—a way of playing he is comfortable with. Whether you realize it or not, you are developing yours.

➤ Principle 155: Know yourself.

That might sound more like something you would hear from your Zen master or your therapist. Believe it or not, knowing who you are is important in bridge as well.

The first step is to be as honest with yourself as you can be. If you allow your ego to dictate your actions at the bridge table, you will always be frustrated. The moments of triumph from ego-driven actions are too rare and fleeting to be a meaningful part of your bridge experience.

That's not to say that your ego should not be involved. It is good for your confidence and feeling of self-worth to strive for improvement and to achieve it.

In assessing yourself for your own purposes, be realistic. It does not reflect poorly on you as a person if others in your bridge circle are more proficient. It is not demeaning for you to seek advice from those with more experience. They are not better than you because they can play the cards more expertly. It is not a reflection on you in any way if you don't know as much as you would like to. You are worthy because you are trying.

♣ ♦ ♥ ♠

A person who thinks he already knows it all has little room for growth.

▶ Principle 156: Ignore the bridge snobs.

Most of the people you meet playing bridge will share with you a deep-seated love of the game. Before you even know their names, they will be kindred spirits. By and large, bridge players are friendly, sociable, and caring. You will be surprised how many of them will be willing to help you when you are just starting out.

A movement in organized bridge that started in the mid-1990s has put a special premium on good behavior. That it was necessary speaks to the problem of the bridge snobs—those who tend to look down on anyone who hasn't achieved expert status. The irony is that few if any of these types are truly experts themselves. They are being weeded out by club owners all across North America, but you may run into one from time to time.

If and when you do, remind yourself that bridge is a great game, that you have met many wonderful people and that one insecure, immature galoot is not going to spoil your fun. You should also report any boorish behavior to the club owner or, if you encounter one of these misfits at a tournament, to the chief tournament director.

♣ ♦ ♥ ♠

Believe in yourself, and no one's doubts will keep you from your goals.

➤ Principle 157: Never show emotion.

In some arenas, emotion can be a vital ingredient to success. If you are the underdog team in a college football game, emotion can carry you to heights you might not ordinarily achieve. A competitor who insults his opponent or takes him for granted is risking a backlash of emotion from the anger he has created in his foe.

It should be noted, of course, that even in physical sports, a cool head is preferred.

In bridge, emotion is appropriate only after the final card of the session is played. At any other time, emotion will do nothing but cloud your mind—and a clear head is an absolute must for success in bridge.

Emotion, of course, comes in many guises at the bridge table. You may be angry at your partner for forgetting part of your bidding system or for failing to give you a ruff. Perhaps you are greatly disappointed in yourself for a bonehead play you just made. You may fear the pair you have just sat down at the table against because they always seem to have your number. You may be gloriously happy that you just executed a squeeze against one of the top players at your club—just the person you wanted to impress.

You must fight to repress all of these reactions, at least while you are playing.

♣ ♦ ♥ ♠

You will always have an advantage if you save
your emotions for the proper settings.

➤ Principle 158: Always bid cheerfully, not matter how dire the situation.

Here is the situation. You are vulnerable, playing in a pair game, and hold the following hand:

♠J643   ♥Q32   ♦1087   ♣943

W	N	E	S
1♠	Dbl	P	?

This is awful. You don't have any suit longer than three cards, except for spades, which your left-hand opponent has opened, indicating at least five.

You can't pass. That shows a boatload of spades—and good ones at that.

There's nothing you can do except bid 2♣, right? Well, that's not exactly true.

If you agonize, hem and haw, run your hands through your hair several times, and finally drag the 2♣ bidding card from the box—or croak out a pitiful "Two clubs"—you might as well be wearing a sign around your neck, saying in big, bold letters: "Double me!"

On the other hand, if you calmly and cheerfully flop the 2♣ bidding card onto the table, seemingly without a care in the world, you will have a chance to get out of this mess. The opponents, after all, cannot see through the backs of the cards. They might well be able to massacre whatever contract you and your partner land in, and they certainly will if you tell them by your demeanor that you absolutely hate your bid. They will miss out a fair number of times, however, when you don't let them in on your secret.

Learn to be at your best when the situation is the worst.

▶ Principle 159: Cultivate a confident bearing.

It's important to project an air of confidence, even if you don't necessarily feel that way. Think about how you react when you sit down against someone who greets you cheerfully, pulls his cards out of the tray as though he can't wait to get started, doesn't hesitate over his bids, and always seems pleased with the way things are going.

It's more difficult to play against a person like that, isn't it? You're more likely to think the bids and plays he makes are correct—that perhaps he already knows what you hold in your hand. In the aura of someone like that, you feel less certain of your own decisions.

It doesn't have to be that way. You can take steps to project that same aura.

Start by sitting up straight in your chair. Players who slump project uncertainty and a lack of confidence. Always seem pleased to see whomever you are playing against, even if it's your nemesis. Believe it or not, if you project self-assurance, you will have a better chance of breaking that losing streak, which will give you real confidence. Hold your cards up; call the cards from dummy in a crisp, authoritative voice. Don't mumble. Show that you are sure of yourself by complimenting an opponent when he makes a good play. Shrug off bad results. This is another mark of a confident player. You know you will make it up later—no problem.

♣ ♦ ♥ ♠

Confidence is a state of mind.

➤ Principle 160: Be consistent.

Bridge, above all else, is a partnership game. The more you play, the more you will see that the most gratifying moments in the game come from true partnership communication and cooperation. When you and your partner have worked in tandem to defeat a seemingly unbreakable contract, you will feel a thrill unlike any other in the game. It follows, then, that partners are precious commodities in bridge. When you find a partner with whom you are compatible, you want to keep him. One way to do that is to make him comfortable. Players who are comfortable sitting across from you will want to have the experience again.

Being consistent doesn't mean you can't take a position now and then—such as opening 3♦ in third seat at favorable vulnerability with six to the Q-10 and little else. Being consistent doesn't mean giving up creativity altogether. More to the point, it means raising your partner's overcalls when you have a raise, respecting your partner's decision when he declines a game try, adhering to the system you have agreed to play, and making an effort to know the system.

♣ ♦ ♥ ♠

Mutual respect is an absolute necessity for a successful partnership.

▷ Principle 161: Always play tough.

This is another way of saying you should respect the game. Bridge is not Old Maid or War. You have to put something into it to get something out of it. You have to pay attention; you have to study— you have to try.

Yes, in the end it's still just a game, and you can have loads of fun without being a world champion or even an expert, but part of the fun of bridge is appreciating the wonderful complexity and endless variety. You'll never even notice these if you are nothing more than a card pusher.

You want respect at the bridge table. One way to get it is to keep working at it. The players whose respect you want can tell who is trying and who isn't. If you play tough, always working hard to get the most out of yourself, the good players will help you by offering advice and playing with you now and then.

Some people have a natural gift for the game—they can see things at the table, in the heat of battle, others wouldn't notice even with all four hands exposed. Advanced plays are trivial to them.

Chances are you are not one of the gifted few. That's okay. You have lots of company. Fight for your place in bridge. It's worth it.

♣ ♦ ♥ ♠

A humble beginning does not confine you to mediocrity.
If you are determined, you can make your mark.

Chapter 25

Bad Habits—
Always Leave Home Without Them

If you have been playing bridge mostly with the neighbors on Saturday nights, chances are you have acquired some bad habits. It's doubtful you have been in very serious competition, which tends to straighten things out more quickly than less-competitive arenas. "Serious," of course, does not mean unfriendly. The players in a duplicate game are there to compete, but they enjoy the social aspects of the game as well. Bad habits are not the exclusive province of home bridge by any means. You can fall into some traps—and they come in a wide variety—in just about any venue. In the case of these hindrances to your game, an ounce of prevention is worth a pound of cure—maybe more.

> ➤ **Principle 162: Don't get stuck in beginner games.**
It's human nature to take the path of least resistance, but it won't get you where you want to go in bridge.

Most clubs and tournaments have games for newcomers. These games are designed to ease the rookies into the world of duplicate. There are restrictions on bidding systems permitted, and players are all of a similar experience level.

This is a cozy world with no "sharks" or experts to make life difficult.

It's also no place—at least on a long-term basis—for someone who wants to improve.

Your bridge brain is like one of your biceps. If you want to gain strength in your arm, you must push your limits. You might start with a five-pound weight, but if you never picked up anything heavier, you wouldn't progress past a certain point.

To be sure, you will take your lumps if you move from the newcomer game to the open game occasionally, but keep in mind that the players who are putting those knots on your head were in your shoes once themselves. They were inexperienced and got beat up the first time they tried for more, but here they are. Extend yourself now and then and you will soon be one of them.

You can find out a lot about who you are by testing your limits.

▷ Principle 163: Don't be afraid of good players.

The late Barry Crane is widely regarded as the greatest matchpoint player of all time. Those who envied Crane sometimes disparaged him as a "rabbit killer"—a player who preyed on the less-experienced, easily daunted pairs he encountered in the tournaments he attended. Such musings were mostly sour grapes—Crane won many national championships in which the fields were very strong. He and Kerri Sanborn (then Shuman) won the World Mixed Pairs in 1978 by a nearly unimaginable margin.

It's true that Crane probably gained lots and lots of matchpoints because of who he was. Everyone knew him, and he made himself visible at tournaments. Many of those who sat down at his table were defeated before they even looked at their hands.

Crane was not the only expert to benefit from this aura of invincibility or omniscience. Many newer players tend to impart these qualities to any good player they encounter. They think that whatever the expert does will be correct and that the expert never makes mistakes.

Don't buy into that.

Good players may not make as many mistakes as those with less experience, but they can't turn your aces into deuces. If you do what is correct with the cards in your hands, there's nothing any player—expert or newcomer—can do about it.

The other point is that good players often make mistakes. In fact, bridge is a game of errors. The players who make the fewest boners normally have the best chance to win, but there probably has never been a session played by anyone with no mistakes. The game just doesn't allow that. It's part of the challenge of the game that it can be difficult in that way.

Look upon your meetings with expert players as an opportunity to learn, not an occasion to dread. If you finish your round against a good player with what seems like a poor result, try to work out later on what went wrong. Many times a good player will be happy to answer your questions after the game.

Above all, concede nothing—and fear no one.

♣ ♦ ♥ ♠

Never pass up an opportunity to learn.

➤ Principle 164: Don't fall in love with certain conventions.

When you first learn about a nifty-sounding convention, it's natural to want to trot it out the first chance you get. One of the most abused is the Unusual 2NT, typically employed when an opponent opens one of a major. A direct overcall of 2NT shows 5-5 or better in the minors and generally a weakish hand—at least in terms of high-card strength—but two decent suits.

This can be an effective weapon when your partner has lots of one of the minors, but you must balance this against the information it provides to the opposition should they end up winning the auction.

The Unusual 2NT is not the only abused convention. The Michaels cuebid is another. It, too, shows 5-5 distribution, in the majors or in a major and a minor. As with the Unusual 2NT, you must be judicious in the use of this convention because of the dangers involved and because of the information you give up.

You may also be tempted to overuse your system for bidding when the opponents open a strong 1NT. The same dangers lurk.

The point of all this is that misusing—or simply overusing—conventions is one of the easiest habits to fall into. Have a plan when you enter the auction. Don't do it just to hear yourself speak—or to try out your gadget.

Acting without a plan will result in wasted effort.

▷ Principle 165: Avoid getting into a doubling rhythm.

There will be many times when you will have the opponents on the run. Perhaps an opponent has made a vulnerable overcall and you lie in wait with a big trump stack. When you and your partner agree to play negative doubles, you cannot make a penalty double directly. You must pass and rely on your partner to "double back in," a takeout measure that you plan to convert to penalty.

♠QJ87   ♥85   ♦Q10953   ♣K4

W	N	E	S
	1♥	2♦	P
P	Dbl	P	P
Redbl	P	3♣	?

If you allow yourself to get into a doubling rhythm, you will feel like once you got the opponent on the ropes, clearly where you had him in 2♦ doubled, you're going to punish him and collect your big penalty. After all, he is now a level higher.

The trouble is, you don't have good enough trumps to be doubling a club contract. Remember, your tricks as a defender on a deal like this one come from trumps—not points.

It might seem that the opponents are jumping from the frying pan into the fire, but you have to have trump tricks to make that reality.

Happiness comes with accepting that you can't have everything.

➤ Principle 166: Don't double out of spite.

If you play bridge long enough, it will happen to you. The opponents will find a fit but stop short of game, perhaps in a competitive auction, but not necessarily. You or your partner will take some action to try to boost them up a level. The result will be that the opponents will find new life and, to your utter chagrin, bid the game they stopped short of moments before.

W	N	E	S
1♠	P	2♠	P
P	3♣	3♠	P
4♠	P	P	?

Your emotions will tell you this is impossible. They couldn't bid past 2♠ a minute ago and now they're in game! Someone's going to pay for this! You might even be steaming because your partner gave them another chance, darn him! Your natural tendency is to exact the maximum penalty by doubling the fools.

Be careful here. Unless you have a trump stack, if you double, you could be turning an average score into a zero. Clearly the opponents made a mistake, either by passing 2♠ initially or going on to game after your partner balanced. It may not be apparent which, so take it easy.

♣ ♦ ♥ ♠

It is rarely a good idea to react to an impulse.

▷ Principle 167: Don't try to make up for a disaster.

Bridge is full of surprises. The more you play, the more you will be amazed at the range of possibilities.

Some of the surprises will not be welcome. Inevitably, you will suffer major reverses, often described in the vernacular as disasters.

These can take many forms. You make a silly bid and suffer a huge penalty; you take your eye off the ball just for one second and let the opponents make a contract with no legitimate chance; you have a bidding misunderstanding and land in a slam, missing the ace and king of your trump suit. The list could go on and on, but count on it: You will eventually suffer some calamity. If you play long enough, they will be legion.

When disaster strikes, your reaction will say a lot about your development as a player.

If you can laugh it off, you're heading for a long and successful playing career. If you can't do that now, at least file it away for consideration later.

Above all else, follow this rule about coping with disaster: Don't try to make up for it. If you do, you will likely have two disasters to overcome, and the effect can be devastating to your current session or, worse, to your partnership.

♣ ♦ ♥ ♠

Losing one battle does not mean you have lost the war.

▶ Principle 168: Don't give unsolicited lessons.

At some point, your competence and your confidence will begin an upward progression. You will spot your own and other players' errors more easily, your postmortem analysis will be more accurate, and you will begin to see things in a different light.

It is natural to want to "share" your revelations with the bridge world at large, sometimes by offering lessons to your partner and to the opponents.

These "gifts" are rarely welcome, and you do yourself no favors when you let fly with a faulty analysis.

Even if you are correct, however, unless someone asks, keep your mouth shut. It embarrasses everyone at the table when you make pronouncements as to how a failed contract could have been made or how a better opening lead would have sunk a contract that made.

Apart from issues of courtesy and good sportsmanship, free lessons also slow down the game.

♣ ♦ ♥ ♠

Let your actions do your talking.

Chapter 26

Keeping Your Mind in the Game

To be successful at bridge requires an array of skills and attributes. Perhaps the most important is the ability to concentrate. This is true, of course, in just about any competition. From baseball pitchers to golfers, the ability to focus is an indispensable part of the makeup of a winner. In bridge, failure to maintain focus can be devastating. It is said that when a bridge player is truly concentrating on his play, he wouldn't notice a naked woman if she walked by his table. Such a stunt was actually pulled off at a tournament many years ago, and the expert in question saw nothing but the cards.

➤ **Principle 169: Conserve your mental energy whenever you can.**
A person who has spent several days at a bridge tournament will feel like he has run a couple of marathons when it's all over. Maintaining concentration for three and a half hours at a time, twice a day or more for up to six or seven days can leave you totally exhausted. It's no wonder that many professional players spend time working out to get themselves into top physical shape. They can't afford letdowns brought on by fatigue.

Understand, also, that you can't turn concentration on whenever you think it's needed. The truth is that it's necessary just about all the time. You must watch the spot cards, your partner's as well as the opponents'. You must take note when someone shows out of a suit; you must count continually. If you are not concentrating, you will miss obvious lines of play or defense. You will "wake up" in the middle of a deal and wonder what cards your partner has been playing. You will realize you have no idea what is going on.

You probably will not be able to maintain concentration for an entire session. There will be distractions, such as a director call or a spilled cup of coffee. Thoughts will come unbidden into your head: what to have for dinner, whether to buy a new car, lots of different things. You will give yourself a better chance for maximum concentration—within your ability, anyway—if you conserve your mental energy whenever you get the chance.

The best opportunity will be when you are dummy. Practice taking a mental break from the game to recharge your batteries, even if it's just a small amount. Do not try to follow the play. Let the other three players do what they will (in duplicate, you will have to play the cards your partner calls, but that doesn't require much mental energy).

Try to forget about what has happened so that you can focus on what's to come. The deals already played cannot be changed. Don't waste mental energy worrying about them.

♣ ♦ ♥ ♠

It is a complete waste of energy to worry about what cannot be changed.

➤ Principle 170: Do your best to eliminate emotion from your game.

An emotional reaction to a disaster can lead to another disaster. If you are angry at your partner or upset with yourself, it is unlikely you will be able to focus on the job at hand, be it playing a contract or defending one—even making rational decisions in the bidding.

The negative emotion of anger is not the only danger, however. When something good happens at the table, it can also interfere with your concentration. Let's say a pair who routinely clean your clock have just bid a grand slam that depended on a finesse—and it failed. If you are mentally shouting hurrah and chortling to yourself, you will not be able to focus on what's coming next.

Perhaps you just got off to a brilliant opening lead, defeating a contract that almost certainly will be made at every other table. If you are still congratulating yourself on your coup, how can you give full attention to the next deal?

A rush of emotion often comes unbidden. You can't control these reactions. It's normal to be happy or angry or frustrated. What you must work on is not letting these concentration killers into your head.

Cultivate a calm demeanor. Don't get too high over your successes or too low when things go badly. When you feel that emotion welling up inside you and threatening to steal your mental energy, take a deep breath. At your first opportunity, get up and get a glass of water or a cup of coffee—or go check last week's scores on the bulletin board. Do whatever it takes to stop that feeling from taking over.

♣ ♦ ♥ ♠

Life + perspective = contentment.

> **Principle 171: Let go of what has already happened.**

Playing good bridge is tough. You have to cope with contentious opponents, keep track of the cards that are played, draw inferences, match bids and plays to the appropriate situations. It's a seemingly endless list.

The most difficult of the tasks you will face is also one of the most important: Once you have played a hand, let it go—*really* let it go. That means don't think about it at all while the session is in progress.

This is so difficult to do because you make such an investment in each and every deal that it seems unnatural to just cast it aside. Still, it's an absolute must.

If you are thinking about your rotten luck on the previous deal—*Why do trumps always break like that for me?*—you cannot possibly give your full attention to what you are doing right at the moment, and that's all that really counts.

Okay, you made a bonehead play. Can you possibly imagine that fretting over it will change anything?

One of the key differences between the world champions and those who aspire to such status is that the veteran players relegate their disasters and triumphs to the past.

One of the advantages of playing duplicate is that you can mark your scorecard to review a particular board after the session. This should help you remove it from your thought cycles for the present.

♣ ◆ ♥ ♠

You cannot change your past, and you should not allow it to ruin your present.

➢ **Principle 172: Forget about being fixed.**
One of the attractions of bridge is the broad range of possibilities. If you play enough, you will find yourself in many interesting situations. You will also discover that the game can be utterly frustrating. You might as well get used to the idea of being fixed. It's going to happen.

Fixes take many forms.

♠J1076   ♥74   ◆A654   ♣832

W	N	E	S
		1NT	P
3NT	All Pass		

You start with a low spade—a logical choice since West didn't use Stayman—and the following turns out to be the entire deal.

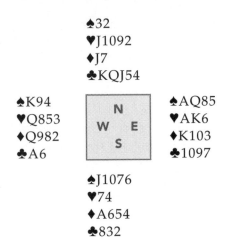

♠32
♥J1092
♦J7
♣KQJ54

♠K94
♥Q853
♦Q982
♣A6

♠AQ85
♥AK6
♦K103
♣1097

♠J1076
♥74
♦A654
♣832

East, using the Rule of 11, puts in dummy's ♠9, which holds. He then plays a diamond to his king and your ace (you could make the deceptive play of ducking, but it's not going to help your score—declarer already has nine tricks now). You get out with a club, but declarer wins the ace, cashes three hearts and three more spades, finally leading the ♦10 to dummy's queen (afraid to finesse because the club suit is now wide open). *Voilà!* The ♦J falls and you can kiss all the matchpoints on this deal goodbye. East has just taken eleven tricks.

What a massive fix! Most players holding the West hand would bid 2♣ to see if East had a four-card major. That would give North a chance to double 2♣ to indicate a strong holding in that suit. Since no major-suit fit would be found, the contract would still be 3NT, but instead of leading a spade and giving up a trick, you would start with a low club and declarer would be doomed. Declarer could duck, but North would be able to knock out the

♣A while you still have a club to play to him. Neither major suit breaks, so declarer would have to go after diamonds. You would win the ace and play your club. You would take at least five tricks on defense, possibly six if either of you has a good major suit to cash when you get in.

This kind of thing will happen to you from time to time. It will grate on you, and you will want to say something nasty to the opponents whose poor bidding turned out so richly for them.

Don't let these things get to you. The proper way to think about this is that opponents who bid this way will probably give you more good results than bad. Accept that occasionally they will profit from their silly bidding. If you stew over fixes, you will have bad results that have nothing to do with the opponents' actions.

♣ ♦ ♥ ♠

When Dame Fortune smiles on another,
be happy for the recipient. You could be next.

➤ Principle 173: Don't play too fast.

It is a good idea to try to emulate the good players you meet at the table. You can learn a lot from studying their habits and their mannerisms.

There is one trait of many experts that you are better off leaving to them, however. Careful observation will reveal that many expert players are very fast in their play. Situations that make others pause are familiar to them from repeated exposure. They know what to do and they get on with it. Not every expert plays in this fashion, but many do.

When you are trying to establish yourself, do not put a premium on rapid-fire play or bidding. Sacrifice a little in the "looking cool" department to get a good handle on what you're doing. You will eventually function more smoothly at the table, but it takes time and patience. In fact, most expert players will tell you that more contracts are lost from playing too fast at trick one than at any other point in the play.

Here's one caution that could save you a lot of anxiety: Even if a play seems overwhelmingly obvious, take one more look—consider it one more time. You will thank yourself on the occasions, rare though they may be, when you avert a crucial mistake.

Look before you leap.

▶ Principle 174: Don't play too slowly.

You get no extra credit for making decisions extra quickly. Putting a premium on speed for speed's sake merely increases the likelihood of mistakes.

Having said that, you must avoid a glacial pace at the bridge table. It is inconsiderate to hold up the progress of the game (nearly all of which have strict time limits)—and it drives your partner crazy, especially if you are slow to make plays as a defender.

It's good to try to think things through and process the available information to figure out the right line of play or defense, but if you're still stuck after a minute or two of deliberation, give it up. Do the best you can and get on with the game. If the problem is particularly knotty, plan to retrieve the board when the game is over and try to determine where you went wrong (if you did—the play you finally made might well have been the correct one).

Refusing to make a decision is a decision.

▶ Principle 175: Train yourself to watch every card.

Here's a true story to show you how the minds of some bridge players work. In 1978, a player from Toronto named Wayne Merkel played in a major team event against a professional player from

Texas named Mike Passell. They faced each other in a seven-board match in Merkel's home town.

On one deal, Merkel opened a weak 1NT (12–14 high-card points), was doubled by his left-hand opponent, and played it there. He went down five tricks.

Later in the match, he opened 1NT again. This time his right-hand opponent doubled, and he played it there again—down five a second time.

Fast-forward to a major bridge tournament in New Orleans in the fall of 2003, more than twenty-five years later.

Merkel and Passell faced each other again in a team event, this one of slightly longer duration. At one point, Merkel's partner opened 2♣, showing a very strong hand. Merkel bid 2♥, a convention showing an extremely weak hand. As it happened, his partner had a lot of hearts, so he ended up playing in 4♥, again doubled. He went down four.

When the play was finished, Passell leaned over and spoke so that only Merkel could hear. Passell said, "Wayne, you're getting better."

If it seems remarkable that Passell could remember the two deals from twenty-five years previous, bear in mind that many expert bridge players can remember exact spot cards from deals played decades in the past.

Now, it's not necessary for you to be able to recall hands from yesterday, or even earlier in the session, but you should train yourself to watch *every* card played during *every* deal. It is a miserable feeling to find yourself in the middle of the play of a contract and realize you don't remember what your partner played a couple of tricks earlier. It is especially discouraging when you realize he was signaling to you in that suit. If you can't recall the card, you don't know whether, at this point, you should or should not play that suit.

One memory aid you can practice is to mentally "say" each card to yourself as it appears on the table. Doing so will give you a fighting chance to remember it later. Of course, you can't "say" the card to yourself if you don't look at it.

♣ ♦ ♥ ♠

You can only learn from the past if you are able to remember it.

➤ Principle 176: Don't let bad cards take your mind out of the game.

No matter what form of the game you play, there will be times when you have a run of cards that look more like tram tickets. The beauty of duplicate bridge, the best form of the game, is that you can win even with bad cards.

But only if you keep your mind in the game.

It's easy to sit there looking at a bunch of 3s and 4s and 7s, thinking that you can't wait until the deal is over so you can get back into the game. That is a losing attitude.

You will have this experience almost exclusively when you are a defender. When you are dummy, remember, you aren't watching what's going on, and when you are declarer, you are—or better be—very much involved, no matter how bad your hand is.

There are ways you can contribute even if you don't take any tricks. You can signal your count in a certain suit to help partner figure out the distribution of the enemy cards. If your hand is truly bad, chances are your partner already knows it. He's counting the cards, after all, and if you're completely broke, he's probably looking at a few face cards, so he knows the score. You might be able to falsecard against declarer by indicating some holding your partner knows you can't have. It might fool declarer and send him on the wrong path.

Then there will be times when you actually do have trick-taking potential even if it's not readily apparent. You must be ready for those occasions.

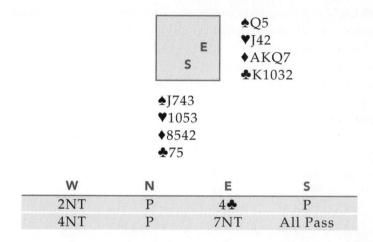

	♠Q5
	♥J42
	♦AKQ7
	♣K1032

♠J743
♥1053
♦8542
♣75

W	N	E	S
2NT	P	4♣	P
4NT	P	7NT	All Pass

East's 4♣ was the Gerber convention, asking about aces. When West showed three aces, East took a shot at the grand slam. The 2NT opened showed 20–21 HCP.

Your partner, North, leads the ♣10, taken in dummy with the queen. Declarer follows with the ♣6.

Declarer considers his next play carefully before playing a heart to the ace, a heart to the jack, then another heart to the king in his hand. When declarer plays the ♥Q, your partner discards the ♠2. Declarer pitches a low club from dummy, and it's your turn.

It seems normal to discard from the weak diamond holding, and it goes against the grain for you to pitch from an original holding of four to the jack. Can you read anything into partner's spade discard? If you are paying attention, you will know that your partner is showing you what is known as "current count." If he had started with three spades, he would play the highest one left—the ♠9 if his original holding had been ♠1092. With an original holding of ♠10982, he would play the ♠2 because he had three left. He will make this discard because your signal at trick one (♠7) told him what he needed to know—that declarer started with only three spades and therefore can never take more than three tricks in the suit.

You won't know that your partner is helping you out, however, if you aren't paying attention and you might instinctively hold on to the wrong card. If you thoughtlessly discard from your seemingly worthless diamond holding, however, you will make declarer very happy if the full deal is as follows:

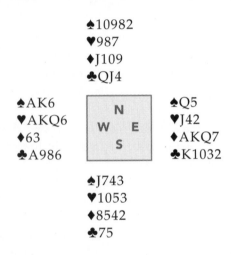

♠10982
♥987
♦J109
♣QJ4

♠AK6
♥AKQ6
♦63
♣A986

♠Q5
♥J42
♦AKQ7
♣K1032

♠J743
♥1053
♦8542
♣75

A diamond discard from you would make dummy's ♦7 the thirteenth trick. Are you prepared to explain to your partner that you weren't paying attention to his signal? You might be faced with a decision such as this without the benefit of a helpful signal from your partner. If you just don't know what to do, here's one way to make your decision: Keep what you can see. In other words, you don't know what declarer has in spades in his hand, but you can see four diamonds in the dummy—and you can beat one of them.

♣ ♦ ♥ ♠

You owe it to yourself to do your best at all times.

Chapter 27

Partnership Care

You cannot be successful in bridge without a partner. It takes four people—two against two—to have a game. Much of what goes on across the table from you will be beyond your control—to a degree, anyway. In the end, however, your actions will have a profound effect on your partner's performance—for good or bad. The key will be the way you behave toward that most valuable person in your bridge life. It's important to practice your bidding and your card play, to strive for excellence for yourself. You will never reach your potential, however, if you don't get the most from your partner.

➤ Principle 177: Make it your nature to nurture.

This doesn't come easily for everyone. Bridge players are a naturally competitive, sometimes contentious lot, who must have tough skin to survive in the fierce arena of a bridge game. You must be tough as nails when it comes to competition and in handling disappointment, but you must also be gentle and supportive.

In the old days of bridge, it was not uncommon to see one player publicly berating another over an error or a disagreement. One of the greatest bidding theorists of his time was known as an absolute monster at the bridge table. Bob Hamman, the world's top-rated bridge player since 1985, describes a partnership from his early playing days as truly miserable. He often had to strain to keep from punching his partner in the nose because of all the abuse he took.

Nowadays, the top players are models of decorum. Close observation reveals that no matter what happens at the table, no one says anything that isn't supportive. If something comes up that requires discussion, it happens when the session is over. The best players of today are also known as the best partners.

If you want respect, you must give respect.

▶ Principle 178: Make the effort to find a compatible partner.

It's interesting how often the term "chemistry" surfaces in discussions of competitive efforts. It's not uncommon for professional sports teams to stand pat at the trading deadline for fear of a negative effect on that nebulous thing called chemistry.

A bridge partnership is no less of a team just because it's only two people. Make no mistake: Compatibility and teamwork are major elements of success.

You can't quantify what makes one pair highly effective, while another—with seemingly equal skills and interest in the game—just never seem to get untracked. There are, however, some identifiable attributes of those who seem made for each other.

First on the list is that they like each other. Successful bridge partnership is more than just sitting across the table from someone for three hours or so. You will spend time discussing bidding systems and going over the details of the sessions to iron out problem areas. This will be a very difficult chore if you don't like the other person.

Compatibility of style is also important. The players don't have to be alike—a somewhat conservative bidder is actually complemented by one who is on the aggressive side—but they cannot be radically different in approach. This can cause friction, which is damaging to any partnership.

Good partnerships are also in agreement about the general approach regarding the system used, and it's a bonus if both are willing to compromise.

Both players must have a similar level of commitment. If one wants to discuss system only half an hour before game time, while the other wants to maintain a 100-page book of system notes for study and frequent adjustment, there could be trouble.

You won't find a more gratifying and rewarding element of bridge than a smoothly running partnership. If you try out lots of partners in your early development, you have a better chance of finding the one for you.

♣ ♦ ♥ ♠

You are stronger when you have someone by your side sharing your vision and your goals.

▷ **Principle 179: Make sure your partner can trust you.**
It's sad to see a partnership where there is no trust. The lack of trust is manifested in many ways, but usually in the bidding.

Perhaps South holds the following hand:

♠AKJ54   ♥87   ♦J104   ♣Q72

W	N	E	S
		1♥	1♠
2♥	P	P	?

This is a clear-cut pass, particularly if North-South are vulnerable, but you will see some South players bid 2♠. They don't trust their partners to take action with an appropriate hand. South must trust North to have passed for a reason—not from inertia. It's likely that North does not have spade support—and if he does he's flat broke. South must infer that North has remained silent for a legitimate reason.

To earn your partner's trust, you must be consistent in your bidding and honest with your signals.

♠976   ♥Q109   ♦KJ4   ♣7654

You are South.

W	N	E	S
	1♠	P	2♠
P	3♦	P	?

Your partner's 3♦ bid is a game try. You have a mere 6 HCP and very flat shape, so your natural inclination is to decline partner's game try. A bid of 3♠ should be the farthest thing from your mind, however. You must bid 4♠. There is no other choice. Your partner's 3♦ bid isn't asking you how you like your hand. He's asking you if you have diamond values, which you do. If you bid 3♠, your partner will trust you and pass. If you miss a game, the way it happened will damage your partnership.

Trust is an essential element of all good relationships.

▷ Principle 180: Trust your partner.
Trust between partners must be mutual. If you do not feel that you can trust your partner, you will never be comfortable with the action at the table. You will always wonder when he declines your game try whether his decision is correct. If he fails to cuebid, you will have an urge to try one more time yourself. It will be like an

itch you want to scratch but can't reach—and it will interfere with your concentration.

There will be times when you love your hand and, as soon as your partner opens, you're thinking slam. You are South.

♠A4   ♥KQ1098   ♦J   ♣K10973

W	N	E	S
	1NT	P	2♦
P	2♥	P	3♣
P	4♥	P	?

If you even consider taking further action, it's a gross overbid. Your 3♣ was forcing to game, showing a second suit. Your partner's jump to 4♥ says that's where he wants to play. If he had a control-oriented hand—aces and kings—he could have cuebid something. There were lots of bids available. He chose not to make any of them. You must trust that your partner knows what he is doing. Perhaps his hand is the following:

♠QJ10   ♥AJ76   ♦KQ4   ♣QJ5

He liked his hand better once you showed your second suit, but his only ace is in the trump suit—and he has dull shape. He also knows that you are short in diamonds and spades, so his high cards in those two suits are not pulling their full weight.

In any case, you have given your partner information to work with and he has decided what to do. If you bid on, you are telling your partner you don't have faith in his judgment.

If you and your team can focus on the ultimate goal, your individual egos will be less likely to get in the way of success.

▶ Principle 181: Don't steal the dummy.

No two players are alike in ability. Your strength might be in the bidding. Your partner might be a better defender. No doubt one of you will be better at dummy play than the other. If you could somehow arrange for each problem to fall into the lap of the player best equipped to handle it, you would have a great advantage in competition.

It just doesn't happen that way. The cards fall in random order. In the long run, when your side buys the contract, you and your partner will split the dummy-play duties approximately down the middle. That is, unless one of you is what is known as a hand hog or a mastermind. In case you are wondering, both terms are derogatory. It *is* possible to arrange to play more than your share of the contracts, but you have to work at it—to the extreme detriment of your partnership.

A bridge mastermind always bids no-trump first, never listens when partner tries to sign off in a long suit, and goes out of his way to play the contract in *his* suit.

First of all, this kind of activity is bad bridge. Masterminding is making decisions completely on your own without consulting your partner, or ignoring the information that your partner supplies that clearly indicates a different decision should be made.

Beyond being bad bridge, hand hogging and masterminding are very bad for partnership morale. If your partner is less experienced than you, he might not realize what you are doing right away, but eventually he will see that you are maneuvering to do all the dummy play. What do you think that will do to his confidence? What would it do to yours if your partner routinely stole the dummy from you? How long would you want to stay in such a partnership?

♣ ♦ ♥ ♠

Never pass up an opportunity to boost a close associate's confidence.

▶ Principle 182: Make partner happy—lead back his suit.

The phrase "lead back partner's suit" is really a metaphor for understanding how important it is to make sure your partner feels good about playing with you. You want him to be comfortable and confident that you and he are on the same page. He wants to trust you. You can do that by leading back his suit, sometimes literally, sometimes figuratively.

The reference, of course, is to your role as a defender, usually against a no-trump contract. Your partner has made the opening lead in some suit and you are the first to get in. It's a general rule that you should lead back your partner's suit, partly because it's usually correct to do so, but more important because it will make him happy when you do.

If you don't return your partner's suit, it better be because (1) you had only one to start with or (2) it was very right to switch suits.

You will have other chances to do what your partner expects and hopes for, and you should avail yourself of the opportunities. If your partner is giving you a ruff and does so with a clear suit-preference signal, honor it unless there is some manifestly correct reason not to. If your partner signals encouragement in a suit while on defense, lead that suit when you get in unless there is a compelling reason not to.

This is not to say that you should do anything automatically or without thinking. Your partner expects you to count the hands and to think about what you are doing. If you can't find a better plan than what your partner is expecting, however, opt for keeping him happy.

♣ ♦ ♥ ♠

If you make your ego secondary to the team's objective, you will have a better chance of success.

▷ Principle 183: Be supportive when your partner errs.

The world championships in 1993 were played in Santiago, Chile. In the quarterfinal stage, a good U.S. team was playing against an equally strong team from the Netherlands in the quarterfinal round.

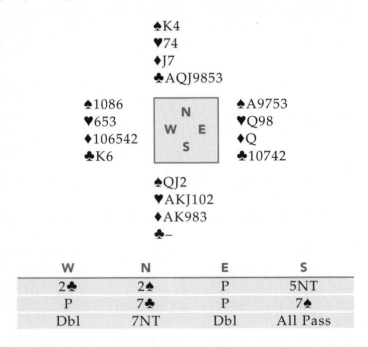

```
                        ♠K4
                        ♥74
                        ♦J7
                        ♣AQJ9853
        ♠1086                          ♠A9753
        ♥653          N                ♥Q98
        ♦106542    W     E             ♦Q
        ♣K6           S                ♣10742
                        ♠QJ2
                        ♥AKJ102
                        ♦AK983
                        ♣—
```

W	N	E	S
2♣	2♠	P	5NT
P	7♣	P	7♠
Dbl	7NT	Dbl	All Pass

The Dutch pair were sitting East-West, the Americans North-South. The two American players were a regular partnership, one of the strongest in the United States.

The auction requires some explanation, of course. In international tournaments, players are allowed to employ some very strange conventions. Many of them are destructive. They serve no purpose but to screw up the auctions of the opponents. The 2♣ opener was one such gadget. It showed a weak hand, usually with a diamond suit.

When you use a convention such as this one, you are required to disclose the method to the opponents and provide suggested defenses. North-South had chosen to employ transfers over the 2♣ opener. Thus North's bid of 2♠ with seven clubs.

Unfortunately, South forgot the agreement about transfers. He thought the 2♠ bid was natural. This is, of course, the kind of thing the East-West pair were hoping for—a major bidding misunderstanding.

South's 5NT bid over 2♠ is the convention known as the Grand Slam Force. It asks the responder to bid seven of the agreed suit if the hand holds two of the top three honors. The North indeed had two of the top three clubs, so he bid the grand slam. The result was the disaster you see in the bidding diagram. 7NT doubled was down three (North-South were vulnerable) for minus 800. At the other table, the Dutch North-South bid to 4♥, a successful contract. It was a 16-IMP loss.

South, although a polished professional player, was beside himself with anguish. This was a disaster of the first order in a very important match.

North, a world champion renowned for his consummate partnership skills, suggested that they take a break to regroup. South, too upset to think rationally, wanted to play on. The final three boards of the set were also bad results.

When the set was over and South was even more distraught than before, North took his partner aside and said calmly, "I love you."

It was the worst moment of North's bridge career, but he could see his partner and friend on the verge of complete self-destruction. Rather than deal in recriminations, North wanted to show that his partner's feelings were more important than what had just occurred.

The team had just suffered a terrible reverse, but the older player understood that berating his partner for the terrible mistake would accomplish only one thing: making his partner more upset.

The U.S. team lost the match in part because of the disaster, but the partnership remained one of the strongest, and they lived to fight another day—and win. The North player, Peter Weichsel of Los Gatos, California, is in the Bridge Hall of Fame today.

This is an extreme example, of course. No game you play in is likely to carry the weight of a world championship match. Nor are you expected to profess your love for your partner when a mistake is made. But you must learn to make it clear you are on your partner's side when things go bad. If your partner makes a foolish play and goes down in a contract you know everyone else will be making, tell him, "Tough luck, partner."

If your partner makes a bid that turns out badly, show some sympathy: "I would have done the same thing, partner."

If you play long enough, you will have sessions that are so bad they'll scare you. If you are lucky, you will have a partner who understands that it's part of the game. He won't abandon you because you had a rough night. He will tell you to go home and forget about it. When the shoe is on the other foot, make sure you remember how your partner treated you.

Another way of looking at this is to be thankful for your partner's mistakes. If he never made an error, he wouldn't be playing with you!

♣ ♦ ♥ ♠

Tough times will help you distinguish between true friends and pretenders.

▷ Principle 184: Avoid conflict at the table.

It's normal for two people, particularly individuals in a long-standing relationship, to have disagreements. You might be fond of a convention your partner would just as soon leave off your card. You might prefer that your partner employ the law of total tricks more often in the bidding. There are any number of areas you will find that require discussion and negotiation.

You might even have some vigorous discussions about any of a number of items each of you feels strongly about.

Just don't have them at the bridge table.

If an area of concern comes up during play, make a note of it for discussion later. If it's absolutely necessary to clear up some point to avoid a problem likely to arise during the session, get it out of the way quickly. Do it partner's way if you must, but take care of it with a minimum of talk.

Two average competitors working in harmony will accomplish more than two stars at odds with each other.

▷ Principle 185: Be a pleasant opponent.

If you're good to your partner, why should it matter whether you are nice to the opponents?

Well, do you think you would function better in an atmosphere with spirited but friendly competition—or one of hostility and rancor? Would you consider it a distraction if your partner never spoke to the opponents or was always at odds with them?

You want your partner to be relaxed so he can use all his mental energy to focus on bridge. You don't want your partner to be upset because of the distraction that comes with that state.

Everything will work better, your mind included, if you foster a relaxed atmosphere. That doesn't mean you won't be trying to take every trick coming to you—plus a few more. No reasonable opponent could take umbrage at that. They're trying to do the same thing to you, after all. If you make them angry, they will try extra hard to beat your brains out. Be nice to them in a social way and they may accidentally be nice to you in a different way.

Never give the opposition an added incentive to get the better of you.

Chapter 28

Growth Patterns

Once you have moved past the learner stage, it will be time to start refining yourself as a bridge player. You are no longer unsure of yourself. You gain confidence every time you play a session, even if it's not a good one. You understand that everything that happens is an opportunity for learning. Aspects of the game that were not so clear six months ago are becoming second nature. You are serious about the game, but your perspective is balanced. It's still just a game and the object is to have fun. You are getting there. Keep trying.

➤ **Principle 186: Form an image of yourself and try to live up to it.**
This may seem fatuous, but a realistic approach to bridge development will aid your quest immeasurably.

If you see yourself as an up-and-coming player rather than someone who already knows it all, it won't damage your psyche so much when the game reminds you, as it certainly will, of all you still have to learn.

If you are honest in assessing your status, you will understand that the winning game you had last night had a lot to do with the accidents the opponents were having and the gifts they were handing out. You will still be aware of the improvements you want to make. You will look back on that game and realize that, if you had performed a bit better yourself, that 63 percent game should have been 67 percent.

If you see yourself as a serious student of the game, you will be humble enough to ask for advice from better players. If this is your picture of yourself and you strive to live up to it, the better players will be pleased to help you. They will see you as a potential future partner.

♣ ♦ ♥ ♠

Be true to yourself.

▷ Principle 187: Don't try to be a genius.

It is natural for bridge writers to chronicle the sensational bids and plays that have amazed observers and competitors through the years. There are indeed some striking examples of genius at work.

Don't try to be one of them—at least not while you're still trying to develop your skills.

It is much more important to focus on solidifying your game and turning yourself into a steady player.

Yes, you will impress your partner and the opponents if you lead the king from ♠K4 out of the blue and hit partner with the ♠A. You will get a ruff—along with some looks (admiration and/ or suspicion). More likely, the impression you leave when your partner turns up with ♠652 will be that you are undisciplined and impulsive. It won't take too many of these misadventures for your partner to be checking out the next table for a new partner.

It could be right, of course, to lead from a doubleton king—for example, if your partner bid the suit or doubled an artificial bid in that suit for the lead.

Bridge has practically unlimited scope for activity by would-be geniuses. Most of them end up looking like fools instead. If you observe good players, you will see that they mostly play straight down the middle. Many of the plays they make in the middle of a contract, either as declarer or a defender, look like "genius" actions but really are the product of deduction and inference from information that has been gleaned through the bidding and play.

Good players don't try for home runs every time they step up to the plate. They know a series of solid singles will do just as well.

That said, here is a brilliantly played deal that might inspire you to greater achievement. It occurred in an Australian tournament. The declarer was Tim Bourke, a fine bridge writer, expert player, and owner of one of the largest bridge libraries in the world. Based on his play, he has studied just the right books.

Study the full deal before reading on to see if you can come up with the winning line of play.

```
                    ♠K108543
                    ♥654
                    ♦J
                    ♣AQ2
        ♠J7            N            ♠Q62
        ♥AJ109      W     E         ♥Q
        ♦875           S            ♦KQ1096
        ♣K765                       ♣J984
                    ♠A9
                    ♥K8732
                    ♦A432
                    ♣103
```

W	N	E	S
P	1♠	P	2♥
P	3♥	P	4♥
All Pass			

Looking at all four hands, it appears that declarer (Bourke was South) has four trump losers. Nevertheless, he brought home the contract.

West led the ♣5. Bourke put in dummy's ♣Q, played a diamond to the ace, and ruffed a diamond. He played a spade to the ace and ruffed another diamond, followed by the ♠K, the ♣A, and a club ruff in hand. Bourke led his last diamond from hand, intending to ruff. Instead, West ruffed in with the ♥9 as Bourke discarded a spade from dummy. The position at that point was as follows:

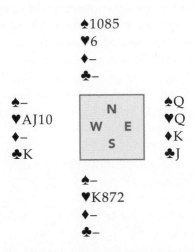

```
            ♠1085
            ♥6
            ♦–
            ♣–

♠–                        ♠Q
♥AJ10        N            ♥Q
♦–        W     E         ♦K
♣K           S            ♣J

            ♠–
            ♥K872
            ♦–
            ♣–
```

West played the ♣K. If Bourke had won the trick in hand, he would have had to lead away from his ♥K, allowing East to win his singleton queen. West would then have taken the last two tricks with the ♥AJ.

Bourke figured out a way to counter the thrust by West. Bourke ruffed the ♣K in dummy with the ♥6 and underruffed in his hand with the ♥2. He was now up to nine tricks. He led a spade from dummy, and when East followed with the queen, Bourke ruffed low. West could do no better than overruff and was then forced to lead away from his ♥A at trick twelve, conceding the tenth trick.

Bourke played brilliantly, but he didn't set out to swing for the bleachers—and he wasn't trying to be a genius. He was simply trying to guard against West's holding length and strength in trumps.

♣ ♦ ♥ ♠

It's good to extend yourself, but be realistic about your reach.

▷ Principle 188: Don't allow other players to dictate tempo.

A common trap for developing players is to let the tempo of a deal get out of hand. The experienced player knows that a rapid-fire series of plays will make it much more difficult for the opponents to avoid errors. Some players just naturally play fast—they process information much more quickly than others. They aren't necessarily trying to intimidate or befuddle the opponents, but it can work out that way.

It's easy for an inexperienced player to fall into the trap of trying to keep up—and that almost always ends up with extra tricks for the expert.

There is no rule or law in bridge that says you must maintain a quick pace in play. It's not polite to take forever, but neither are you obliged to pull your cards with lightning speed.

You will encounter this problem almost exclusively as a defender. It is much easier to control the pace of play when you are declarer.

If you find that the declarer is going too fast for you to keep up, you can ask him to slow it down—or you can simply take your own time. Play must go in rotation, and if it is your turn, no one can preempt that right. Simply stop and take your time.

The main point is to be aware that you are not obliged to play as though the bridge club is on fire, and you should guard against getting caught up in a rhythm that exceeds your ability to process information.

If you don't stick up for yourself, no one will.

➤ Principle 189: Study the laws.

The laws of the game are set up to define correct procedure and to provide a remedy when there is a departure from correct procedure. The laws cover the mechanical aspects of the game, such as clockwise rotation in the bidding, and other matters such as the scoring and rank of the suits.

The laws deal with irregularities, such as leads and bids out of turn, revokes, exposed cards, insufficient bids, and similar procedural foul-ups.

The laws also govern matters such as claims and concessions. There are right and wrong ways to do both—and there are many other similar matters that will arise if you play much bridge at all.

You owe it to yourself to learn as much as you can about the laws. Get a copy and read it. Six months later, read it again.

Remember, too, one of the key mandates of the laws: If an irregularity occurs at a club or a tournament, the director must be called. This is not optional.

Knowledge is power.

➤ Principle 190: Learn mental toughness.

Bob Hamman has been the world's No. 1–ranked player since 1985. He has won nearly a dozen world championships. If you ask him about his greatest asset as a player, he might say it is his mental toughness. An example of his strength took place in a tournament more than twenty years ago. His team was down by a sizable margin as the second half of play began. On the first board of the second half, Hamman and his partner misdefended a doubled contract and let it make. Now they were down even more.

So how did they handle it?

In Hamman's words, "We went on to the next hand."

Of all the players in the world, Hamman is probably best at putting whatever has just happened where it belongs—in the past. He can truly dismiss the result he just achieved at the table—good, bad, or indifferent—and concentrate fully on the hand he just picked up.

You will probably never win a world championship or even contend for one, but you can emulate this quality of one of the greatest players in the history of bridge.

It won't happen without effort, and you won't achieve mental toughness without practice, but if you want to improve your results and your standing among your peers, you must learn to forget about errors—your own and your partner's—and anything else that might distract you.

♠ ♦ ♥ ♠

Change your self-image and you will change your habits as well.

➤ Principle 191: Vow to learn from your mistakes.

Bridge is a game of errors. You can't play without making them, whether you are a beginner or a world champion. In fact, some of the world's greatest players do not consider themselves very good, only "less bad" than others. It's because bridge is enormously—almost unfathomably—complex. It's part of what makes it so fascinating.

It would be a mistake, however, to assume that you cannot enjoy playing unless you can measure up to expert standards. Chances are, the crowd you play in will not be appreciably better than you are, even if you are just starting out. The gap between you and the top player in your club is surprisingly small, and you will realize this the more you learn.

A wise man once said that good judgment comes from experience, and experience comes from bad judgment. Apply this logic to bridge, and use your mistakes to learn. To do so, of course, that means you must recognize your errors, which takes some effort.

The business of having to recognize errors in order to learn may seem like a Catch-22. If you don't know enough to understand when you have made a mistake, how will you ever learn from your errors?

One way to tell is by the scores at the end of the game. Poor scores are usually indicative of a mistake. Some of your zeros will come from brilliancies on the part of the opponents, but your errors will be the source of most of your difficulties. This is why duplicate is so much more interesting and rewarding than party bridge.

♣ ♦ ♥ ♠

Every day brings a new opportunity to learn for those whose minds are open to it.

➤ Principle 192: Be open to new ideas.

In the early days of contract bridge, bidding was simple. Players opened four-card majors, 1NT showed 16–18 HCP, and if you said, "Double," it often meant trouble for the opponents. Only a few conventions were employed, notably Blackwood and Stayman. Some players look on those times as the good old days.

Here's a fact about that time in the annals of bridge: The bidding was terrible.

Today, any player with a few lessons would probably have an advantage in bidding over the experts of the 1920s and '30s, even the '40s. Through the years, there have been many innovations. Al Roth, an expert player and undoubtedly the most original bidding theorist of his time, is responsible for one of the most important inventions in bidding: the negative double.

Virtually no one who plays at a bridge club or in tournaments would consider a bidding system that excluded this convention, yet when it was introduced there was serious resistance.

You no doubt are using many modern conventions: Jacoby transfers over no-trump, for example. This is another innovation with almost complete acceptance. Gaining favor in recent years have been so-called Bergen raises over major-suit openings (indicating at least four-card support for opener).

The list is practically endless. There is a book of conventions that is more than 1,000 pages long.

As you move up the bridge ladder, you will be introduced to many new concepts. Your partners may push you to try out some of the latest ideas (there are always lots of them). Don't dismiss them out of hand. You don't want to overload yourself to the point that you can't remember everything, but you will miss out on one of the more interesting aspects of bridge if you never try anything new.

No boundaries can hold back a strong imagination.

Chapter 29

Honor the Game

Part of your growing-up process in bridge will involve learning about ethics and etiquette at the table. If you are an ethical player, you will not want what is not yours. If the opponents erroneously write up your score as plus 170 instead of the plus 140 you actually achieved, you will tell someone as soon as you notice and get it corrected. If you overhear conversation about an odds-on grand slam on board such and such, and you haven't played it yet, you will tell the director about it. If your partner makes a revealing hesitation in the bidding, you will bend over backward not to take advantage of information you are not entitled to. If an opponent is holding his cards in such as way that you can see them all, you will tell him to pull them back. You want to win, but you want to earn it fair and square. You may not be an expert player, but you are serious about the game and you want to be known as an ethical player. That is the highest compliment anyone can pay.

➤ **Principle 193: Fully disclose your methods.**

Critics of the principle of full disclosure often draw the comparison between bridge and football. In bridge you are required to fully inform the opponents of the bidding system you are using and to explain any of your bids whenever you are asked. Contrast this to football, the critics say. On the gridiron, the Green Bay Packers are not required to tell the Dallas Cowboys that a pass play is coming up. How silly for bridge to require basically the same thing.

The problem with the analogy is that it is not a fair comparison and completely misses the point.

Any bid or call in bridge can be assigned any meaning. The partners simply have to agree on what the bids mean. For example, a 2NT opening bid in most bidding systems shows a balanced hand with 20–21 high-card points. If you play a strong club system, however, all your strong hands come under the umbrella of the 1♣ opener, so you can use other bids in whatever manner you like. So a pair playing a strong club system could decide that a 2NT opener shows a hand with at least five cards in each minor and 4–8 HCP. Or they could use 2NT to show both majors. The possibilities are nearly endless.

So here you are at the table.

♠AJ4   ♥QJ9543   ♦A53   ♣Q

Your right-hand opponent opens 2NT. What do you do with the hand above? Well, you can't decide unless you know the meaning of 2NT. If it's 20–21 balanced, you have nothing to say. Between you and the opener, nearly all the high cards are accounted for. Partner has a weak hand, so you want to stay out of the auction.

But what if 2NT is the very weak hand with lots of minor-suit cards? Well, you would want to get in there. Your partner could well have enough for you to make a game.

Let's say the opponents are not required to disclose their methods. When East opens 2NT, West knows what it means, but North-South do not. If 2NT is the weak hand with minors and the vulnerability is favorable, West might pass because he knows that even if his partner goes down six or seven tricks undoubled, it's still less than the vulnerable game your side almost surely can make.

You can see this is an impossible situation. It's completely chaotic.

You can also see why the comparison to football and the disclosure of particular plays is inappropriate. There is disclosure in football. Certain formations are indicative of running plays; others make it clear a pass is in the offing. To play football completely without disclosure would require the defenders to keep their eyes closed until the ball was snapped.

Whether you like it or not, full disclosure is the law in bridge. You are not allowed to have secret agreements. The winners are supposed to earn their victories by good bidding, good play, and a reasonable amount of luck—not because the opponents were flummoxed and confused by the bidding system deployed against them.

The playing field must be level. Fairness must be maintained.

Remember, also, that just because you must disclose your methods does not mean they will be easy to deal with. An opening bid of 3♠ is still difficult to cope with even if you know exactly what it means.

♣ ♦ ♥ ♠

A victory not honestly earned is as hollow as a long-dead tree.

➤ Principle 194: Learn about ethics.

It is interesting to note that the laws of bridge do not address cheating. It was considered distasteful to give cheaters any status at all, so the issue is not discussed in the laws. That is not to say, however, that the laws contain no mention of the need for proper behavior. In fact, there is an extensive section on the so-called proprieties.

The distinction between breaches of the proprieties and outright cheating is easy to make by citing a couple of famous cases of the latter.

In the 1965 world championships, two British players were accused of relaying information about the heart suit by means of finger signals. In 1975, two Italian players in the world championships in Bermuda were caught tapping their feet together under the table. Neither case was brought to a definitive conclusion, but the accusations were as serious as you will find in the game of bridge.

Players who are caught and convicted of outright cheating are suspended and in many cases expelled. Cheating, of course, can take many guises but usually involve signals of some sort. One pair expelled from the American Contract Bridge League were sending signals by placing their scoring pencils on the table in different ways. Others have sent information back and forth by means of coughing or clicking cigarette lighters (in the days before smoking was banned at most tournaments).

These reprehensible activities differ markedly from breaches of the proprieties.

For example, if your left-hand opponent opens 1NT and your partner goes into the tank, finally emerging with a pass, whether you like it or not, you are now in possession of unauthorized information. After all, was your partner studying for so long because he had a bad hand? Because he had a seven-card suit and a couple of aces? No, it was because he had a hand with moderate values. He wanted to act, but he didn't know what to do.

If your partner had passed without a major pause—in tempo—you could surmise if the opener's partner also passed that your partner had something. His break in tempo acted as confirmation of this. The fact that the information is made available is not a breach in and of itself. What is improper is for you to take advantage of it.

The proprieties cover much more than unauthorized information and hesitations. For example, you are prohibited from conveying information by means of your tone of voice or by frowning or otherwise exhibiting disapproval at a bid or play; you may not deceive an opponent by the manner in which you make a bid or play (deceptive bids and plays in and of themselves are entirely proper); you are required to treat your partner and the opponents with courtesy and respect; partners are not permitted to have undisclosed agreements.

The list is long, but you get the idea. You must play fair. It's that simple.

One bad act can undo everything you have done to build your reputation.

▷ Principle 195: Know your system.

If you choose to play a complicated, convention-laden bidding system, you owe it to yourself, your partner, the opponents, and the game in general to know what you are doing. There are few events in bridge more frustrating—to everyone, of course, but mostly to your partner—than a forgotten agreement or a flawed explanation of an agreement. It smacks of unethical behavior if, when asked about a bidding agreement by an opponent, your only response is "I don't know."

World champion Bobby Wolff is a stickler for ethics, especially in bidding. At one time, he succeeded in promulgating a concept called "convention disruption." The idea was that if you and your partner were playing methods that were constantly being fouled up, creating havoc for the opponents and endless director calls, you were subject to penalty. This idea was popular among two groups. The less-experienced players who are often intimidated by esoteric systems and frequent interruptions in the auctions for explanations, and the serious players who feel the "forgotten" agreements and bids truly disrupt the game and skew the results.

Your actions, not your words, define your character.

➤ **Principle 196: Know when being a "good sport" is wrong.**
Many players find it distasteful to gain from a mechanical error or from an opponent's infraction that does not affect the outcome of a deal.

Here's an example. Say you are playing in a 4♠ contract, and at one point you are running winners in diamonds—a side suit. One of your opponents fails to follow to one of your diamond leads even though he has a diamond. This is discovered after a play to the next trick has occurred, making the play an established revoke.

Your opponent does not win the trick on which he revoked, but his side does win a later trick with an ace (you could not avoid that loser). The laws dictate a one-trick penalty. In other words, if the final outcome of the contract was 4♠ making for plus 420, the score you now receive will be 4♠ with an overtrick for plus 450.

Perhaps you feel that you do not deserve that trick, so you want to waive the penalty. The laws very plainly prohibit you from doing so.

You feel that it would be unsporting to accept a trick you didn't really earn. In fact, it is unsporting to turn it down.

Paying attention is an important part of the game. If your attention lapses and you make a mistake, sometimes you are lucky and get away with it. Other times you will pay in one way or another.

Suppose on the same deal your opponent had simply made a very bad discard and you ended up with the same overtrick because of his sloppy play. Would you also want to give that trick back as well? It is wrong to play God in this way. It is not up to you to decide who should pay for errors and who should not, especially when the laws are specific about what constitutes an irregularity and prescribes the penalties.

Errors of this kind occur all the time. Whether someone pays for his mistake should not depend on which table he is sitting at—yours or that of someone who is more tuned in to the importance of following the rules.

Many players believe the penalties for revokes (if you win the trick on which you fail to follow suit and subsequently win any other trick, it's a two-trick penalty) are truly draconian. Until the laws change, however, you must follow them. You do not have the right to waive any penalty associated with a revoke.

There are occasions, however, when magnanimity is appropriate. For example, many players using bidding boxes pull the wrong card out occasionally, "bidding" something they had no intention of doing. It is sporting, and within the rules, to allow the person to change the bid he clearly did not intend to make.

Without laws, there is chaos.

➤ Principle 197: Don't psych.
Your partner and the next player have passed and you are sitting in third seat with a truly terrible hand.

    ♠J5   ♥106543   ♦Q76   ♣532

Wouldn't it be clever to open that hand 1♠? How would the next player deal with it if he held something like the following collection?

    ♠KQ1098   ♥K   ♦K43   ♣J876

Your bid—known as a psychic—would most definitely make life difficult for the opponents. They might never recover.

Here's another one.

    ♠653   ♥J2   ♦AJ107654   ♣9

Your opponents are vulnerable and you are not. Your right-hand opponent, the dealer, opens 1♥. Wouldn't it be fun to over-call 1NT? Never mind that the bid shows many more high-card points than you have—plus balanced distribution. If they double, of course, you have a place to run.

Psychic bids—a bid that grossly misstates either high-card strength or suit distribution—are perfectly legal. It is within the rules and ethical to try to trick your opponents in this way.

It's best, however, if you forget about psyching before you even start.

These concepts are important: partnership trust, consistency, and honorable behavior. Once you begin a pattern of psyching, you are in danger of violating these principles and hurting your reputation.

While the rules permit psychic bidding, it does not permit you to install a safety net. After all, when you open the bidding 1♠ on a doubleton jack, there is some risk that your partner will raise you and the opponents will work out what has happened and begin to double. Now your imaginative bid doesn't seem so clever, does it? The safety net could take the form of psychic controls: a bid that checks to see if you really had your opener or were just kidding. The problem is that psychic controls are strictly prohibited.

A psychic bid is legal only if your partner is fooled just as much as the opponents.

If you are fond of making psychic bids, pretty soon your partner is going to start making allowances for them. Clear-cut raises by your partner will turn into passes. Jump raises will turn into single raises.

You can see that this will hamper your bidding, but it's also against the rules. It means that your partner is "reading" your psychics. He will begin to know when you are psyching and pull back in the bidding. You may not have a formal agreement with your partner regarding psychic controls, but all your partner's adjustments will amount to the same thing. This is illegal—and unethical.

♣ ♦ ♥ ♠

If you always tell the truth, you won't have
trouble recalling your previous statements.

➤ Principle 198: Play it straight.

You will have some nights at the bridge table that will test your mettle. You will feel as though Murphy's Law—if anything can go wrong, it will—was formulated with you in mind.

So you make some crazy bid, hoping to stir things up, and you go down 1100 against at most a part score for your opponents. Okay, bad board for you, top for them. Who did it hurt?

Well, think about this scenario. You are neck and neck with another pair entering the last round of the event. When the scoring is done, you find out that you have lost because the pair you were competing against faced two players on the final round who were having a miserable game and decided to go crazy, making ridiculous bids that simply handed two top scores to the pair you were trying to beat. Your competitors didn't win because of skill or even luck. They won because they happened to be playing against two irresponsible players. Would you want to win because of some nonsense like that—or would you prefer to earn it?

It is not fair to the field to be taking shots like this all over the room. It skews the results, and unfairly distributes tops and bottoms around the room. Actions such as these can result in your expulsion from a tournament or a club.

Note that irresponsible actions such as these are considerably different from a rational decision to play for a top or bottom, as in taking a backward finesse or in eschewing a safety play to try for extra tricks. These are reasonable gambles, not insane flights of fancy.

♣ ♦ ♥ ♠

If a job is worth doing, do it well or not at all.

> **Principle 199: Set a good example.**

You may not realize it, but people are watching when you play bridge, especially at the local bridge club. One never knows when it might be necessary to recruit another partner or put together a team not to mention the fact that most bridge players are social by nature.

If you play regularly, you will soon be part of the group and possibly a role model for other new players as they come along. It is important, therefore, for you to develop good habits for the time when others are looking up to you.

You are in complete control of your own actions, but you have only limited control over others. You can, of course, influence others by the example you set.

Always play your best, be friendly and respectful to your partner and the opponents, play honorably and ethically, and strive to learn.

You don't have to be an expert or a world champion or even more than an average player. Just try to be the kind of player others will want to grow up to be.

♣ ♦ ♥ ♠

*An unflinchingly positive attitude can overcome
a lot of negative thinking on the part of others.*

> **Principle 200: Give back to the game.**

Bridge is a game you can play for a lifetime. There are few physical limitations. Many competitors continue into their nineties and beyond. Even the blind are able to participate and enjoy the wonder of bridge.

There are more than 3,500 bridge clubs in North America and more than a few overseas. No matter where you find yourself, there will be a place for you to play and meet others with a similar love of the game.

You can give back to bridge a variety of ways. One is to volunteer at your club and when the local organization is putting on a tournament. It might surprise you to know that organized bridge runs mainly on volunteers at various levels. The 1,200 or so bridge tournaments that are organized every year happen mainly through the efforts of volunteers. Your local bridge club also depends on the generosity of people who are not compensated with cash for their time.

An even better way to repay the game of bridge is to play with new players. Many of them, as you were, are in awe of this seemingly complex and difficult game. You will meet many players who need the gentle hand of someone with experience to provide reassurance and guidance.

It can be enormously rewarding to play with someone who is eager to learn. You will swell with pride when you see your protégé gaining expertise and confidence. You will be setting an example for other experienced players to follow.

Best of all, your student will remember how much it meant for you to sacrifice your time for him, and he will be more likely to do the same for another up-and-coming player later in his career.

Giving of yourself is the best gift possible.

About the Author

Brent Manley is editor of *The Bridge Bulletin,* the world's largest-circulation bridge magazine, published by the American Contract Bridge League, with headquarters in Memphis, Tennessee. He is the coauthor of two bridge books: the autobiography of the world's No. 1–ranked bridge player, and a book about the Precision bidding system. He also wrote *The Everything® Bridge Book* for Adams Media.